Stuck in the Middle

Helping Adolescents Read and Write in the Content Areas

Donna Hooker Topping

and

Roberta Ann McManus

D1445246

HEINEMANN
PORTSMOUTH, NH

Heinemann
361 Hanover Street
Portsmouth, NH 03801–3912
www.heinemann.com

Offices and agents throughout the world

Library of Congress Cataloging-in-Publication Data

Topping, Donna.
   Stuck in the middle : helping adolescents read and write in the content areas / Donna Hooker Topping and Roberta Ann McManus.
      p.   cm.
   Includes bibliographical references and index.
   ISBN-13: 978-0-325-02146-1
   ISBN-10: 0-325-02146-5
   1. Content area reading—United States. 2. English language—Rhetoric—Study and teaching—United States. 3. Academic writing—Study and teaching—United States. 4. Interdisciplinary approach in education. I. McManus, Roberta. II. Title.
   LB1050.455.T685 2010
   428.0071'2—dc22
                                                      2009046729

Editor: Lisa Luedeke
Production editor: Sonja S. Chapman
Typesetter: Eric Rosenbloom, Kirby Mountain Composition
Interior design: Shawn Girsberger
Cover design: Lisa A. Fowler
Manufacturing: Steve Bernier

Printed in the United States of America on acid-free paper

14   13   12   11   10   MV   1   2   3   4   5

Contents

Acknowledgments

We are blessed to have wonderful teachers in our lives who continue to inspire us with their dedication to students and their storehouse of ideas. Particularly, we thank those whose work we discuss in this book: John Evans, Ken Woodward, Liz Miller, Craig Bradley, Kevin Bower, Kevin Allen, Jen Martin, Marie Cowan, Chris Weaver, Carla Yocom, Sarah Gajeski, Laura Fehrenbacher, and Adrian Lindquist. To those who have attended our workshops and shared their enthusiasm and creativity, we offer sincere appreciation.

Our colleagues with whom we share our professional lives enrich us daily with their enthusiasm, wisdom, and support. Sandy Hoffman, Jane Rudden, Judy Wenrich, Kim Heilshorn, and Lesley Colabucci offer Donna equal amounts of levity and seriousness at all the appropriate times. Roberta has been fortunate to work with a large cadre of supportive administrators, faculty, and staff in her career. Their support and collaboration have been invaluable. These special people know who they are.

Writing for Heinemann has once again been a pleasure and an honor. Lisa Luedeke has been everything a writer could want in an editor. With her ability to grasp both the big picture and the tiniest of details, she has been a wonderfully supportive friend to this book. Alan Huisman's finesse with language and Kate Montgomery's understanding and guidance were also instrumental. Stephanie Turner, Cindy Black, and Sonja Chapman ably shepherded us through the concluding steps of manuscript preparation and book production. We offer high praise and sincere thanks to the folks at Heinemann.

To the thousands of students who have passed through our classrooms over the years, we say thank you for all you have taught us about teaching. You keep us real.

Finally, our families provide us with ongoing support in every area of our lives and have shared the ups and downs of our "writerly" lives with great empathy. To Kathryne Hooker, Allyson and Ed Stallman, and Brad Topping, and to Rhett McManus, Pete McManus, and Mark McManus, and Chris and Kelly Haase we offer our thanks and love.

Foreword

Often when I walk into Lowes Home Center or Home Depot I mentally hyperventilate. My heart skips a beat, and my creative muse goes into happy shock: All those tools and ideas! "Look at those wrenches," I exclaim to my wife. "I bet they could fix a lot of things in our house. And hey, imagine what we could do with that jigsaw over there! Have you ever seen so many pliers in one place?

My imagination launches a rocket of opportunity, and I'm strapped to the tail fin, wondering where my mind should go first, second, and beyond. It's always a 3:1 ratio at these stores: I buy three additional items for every one item on my original list; I get three new ideas for every one idea I had prior to entering.

That's darn close to the feeling I had as I read *Stuck in the Middle: Helping Adolescents Read and Write in the Content Areas* by Donna Topping and Roberta McManus. Wow, so many tools! So many ways to make learning come alive for struggling students and help teachers in their cause! Clear a path—I'm stuffing my shopping cart with all that I see.

As I read these pages, I was reminded of teachers, including myself from time to time, who too quickly blame students for failing to learn, rather than taking on the more difficult task of questioning and building our own instruction. We think we're trying every strategy known to mankind when really we're just exhausting our limited imagination. It's easy to run out of creative teaching juice, particularly when facing diverse needs in our classrooms and mounting district mandates. During these times, we desperately seek an I.V. full of instructional catalysts. Topping and McManus provide this exact stimulus with these innovative and proven strategies from their decades of teaching experience in multiple grade levels. With this book, we will not lack for ideas.

In fact, Topping and McManus not only lay out a plentiful harvest of terrific reading, writing, and vocabulary strategies—they improve upon them. Old chestnuts like SQ3R and QAR are explained well, but each long-standing strategy receives new polish and innovative application. The authors don't settle for simply using ideas from the teacher's copy of the basal text, for example. They show us how to modify them to differentiate instruction, how to ratchet up the complexity or tune it down, how to push students to stand on their mental tip-toes or provide stepping stones to on-grade level proficiencies.

Woven in with these shiny retoolings are brand new strategies for today's students. I can't wait to try "Skim Sandwich," "Text Box and Text Brackets," "Sticking Points," "Vocabulary Circles," and the "WHMS Radio Call-in Show," among many others. The impact of the strategies here is contagious; students unwilling to participate will have a difficult time remaining on the sidelines when they're used.

Drawing upon the wisdom of Rief, Daniels, Lane, Pink, Popham, and many others, Topping and McManus present the latest thinking and pedagogy, and apply it deftly in real classrooms. The book begins with clear standards for teaching excellence. Thankfully, these principles include how to best prepare students' minds for learning—an important aspect of teaching that receives far too little focus in most classrooms. There are powerful twenty-first-century skills promoted here, too, such as teaching students to encapsulate, synthesize ideas, determine salience, think metaphorically, analyze data, and draw upon background information to create new learning. All the while, the authors are mindful of the unique nature of students' development. They show us how to flex strategies to scaffold instruction for specific individual and class needs. What a joy it is to see so many helpful ideas made transparent so that others can implement them as well!

One of the strongest elements of *Stuck in the Middle* is the license the authors give us to teach outside our comfort zone. In several places, the authors humble themselves, sharing experiences in which they knew little about a topic and invited their students to teach them about it instead. Many teachers find themselves in this position, relying on student expertise to figure out ever-changing classroom technology. Here, the authors embrace failure as one of the great teaching tools it is. While a teacher's stumbling with some aspect of teaching, technology, or content can create genuine empathy on the part of their students, it can also convey a simple but powerful truth: if you want to learn something, teach it to another. The authors' students grew as they taught their teachers. A high-five to Topping and McManus for opening themselves to revision like this in front of their students! All students need clear models of how *not* to know something—and handle it with grace.

We all need to laugh at ourselves and with others, and the authors' quick and easy sense of humor is another great strength of this book. Readers will laugh at how one student responded when McManus pointed to her stomach and asked what it was, and at another student's mnemonic devise for remembering the difference between two elements on the Periodic Table, Silver (Ag) and Gold (Au). Woven in with this humor are plenty of fun poems, graphics, dramatic interpretations, and instructional games that will undoubtedly become the highlight of many students' school day.

Thoroughly vetted in their own classrooms, these strategies are for all content teachers, not just teachers of reading and writing. In fact, the book inoculates us against that dreaded disease, *Literacimonodominpathy,* the illness (*pathy*) that some educators suffer that declares reading, writing, and vocabulary instruction (*literaci*) as the exclusive domain (*domin*) of just one (*mono*) educator, the English teacher. We've evolved as a profession beyond this antiquated thinking; we are all reading, writing, and vocabulary teachers. It is not hyperbole to declare that proficiency in these three areas opens—or slams—more doors for students than anything else taught, K–12. Because Topping and McManus are so content-driven, this book provides practical literacy strategies that are usable in all disciplines. They know how to move teachers from simple classroom survival to creating productive, thriving students.

Teachers can be invited or mandated to use literacy strategies in content areas, but we all know the former is more effective than the latter. Through personable writing, experienced insight, and clear directions, Topping and McManus make reading and writing instruction in content areas inviting, effective, and even fun.

Just as we walk through that home improvement store and the ideas start flowing, as we read this book we're reminded: How about some new light bulbs? Here, they are.

—Rick Wormeli
February 2010

CHAPTER

The Nonnegotiables: Six Principles for Teaching

Tommy runs into the classroom. "What are we doing in science today?" He races to his desk, gets out his textbook and notebook, and readies his pencil, eager for class to begin. This happens every day. A seventh grader, Tommy is in a mainstreamed science class for the first time. His tested IQ is in the low-functioning range, his reading level is first grade, he argues that X is not a letter in the alphabet, but he loves coming to science class. He is the most eager learner in the room.

Adrianne reads aloud haltingly and very quietly from her literature anthology. Her classmates and teacher struggle to hear. Despite repeated prodding, Adrianne will not read louder. She has no problem being heard in the lunchroom or in the crowded hallways, though.

Kyle is trying to get his teacher to let him explain the new strain of flu present in their state. He wants everyone to be alert and take precautions. The social studies lesson on latitude and longitude is being held up by his insistence. His classmates, accustomed to Kyle's lectures, roll their eyes. His learning labels read "academically talented" and "Asperger's syndrome." He reads very well when he is focused. When he is not, his comprehension is spotty and incomplete.

Billy's eyes never leave the teacher. He wants to do everything correctly to get the good grades that make him and his parents happy. He is very focused, happy to be in school, and progresses despite his learning disability and difficulty reading.

Deanna is never without a book. She devours Twilight, *reading it in between classes, in the cafeteria, and on the bus. Not so with her history book. She says it's just too hard to understand.*

Ruth turns around and talks to her friends, smiles at the cutest boy in the room, and passes in her homework. As usual, most of it is correct. She reads well, but hates reading the textbook because it is "s-o-o-o-o boring." She has no learning labels. Just a typical hormonal teenager!

Do these students seem familiar to you? Chances are you can substitute names of your own students. They join a cast of millions who bring a range of reading abilities or inabilities, their love or dislike for reading, and their interests and disinterests to our content-area classes. With the new prominence of high-stakes testing, programs in reading and writing proliferate in today's schools. Yet relatively little attention is paid to the application of these processes in the content areas, where students must *use them to learn* every day. Unlocking informational text can be challenging even for the best readers, and the challenge is compounded for those who have difficulty.

Content-area teachers have a unique opportunity to help students not only learn the material but also improve their overall literacy. Over the past thirty years, we have developed and implemented teacher-friendly, student-oriented strategies to help all students learn through reading and writing—strategies we present in this book. In these pages, we share with you ways to differentiate instruction so that all students learn more content, more effectively, while simultaneously improving the reading and writing abilities they bring to our classes.

You may be a beginning teacher, overwhelmed by the newness of everything. Or you may be an experienced teacher, strangled by the time required to lead committees, write curriculum, and mentor new colleagues. Regardless of the stage of your career, if you're a teacher, you're on a never-ending search for ways to reach your students—ways that have passed the test of real teaching, to real students, in real time. You're in luck—you'll find a collection of these strategies here. If you are overwhelmed by the sheer numbers of students and learning styles, if you need help differentiating your instruction, if you want to know how to help struggling readers learn content, or if you are just looking for new ideas to add to your repertoire, this book is for you

■ The Nonnegotiables

As we develop our teaching craft, we filter everything through six guiding principles—our "nonnegotiables." These principles are derived from our experience, our years of talking about what we believe, and our research into what works for other teachers. Here they are:

1. *All* students can learn.

2. *All* students need good teaching (both content and process).

3. Instruction needs scaffolding.

4. What happens before, during, and after lessons needs to be rethought—and prethought.

5. Teachers need to do whatever it takes.

6. Teachers need to learn from students, not just teach them.

All Students Can Learn

We believe that *all* people can learn. They just can't learn in the same way on the same schedule. It's so easy for teachers to forget this. When we were students, many of us found school to be a series of successful experiences, so much so that we decided to spend our careers there. Learning subject matter through reading and writing came easily, for the most part. It's hard for us to fully understand what it's like for those who have difficulty.

One of the most humbling experiences we have had as adults has been learning and keeping up with new technology. Our false starts and missteps have taught us a lot about teaching and learning and are a reminder of how difficult it can be to learn something challenging. Donna recalls burning a CD for the first time:

> I had some pictures to share and a friend said, "Just burn a CD." "Hmmm," I thought, "well, I know that a CD can mean one of those shiny little disks or it can mean certificate of deposit. Probably it's the former. And burn. Fire? Smoke? Heat? Can't be." I looked at all the icons dancing around the edge of the computer screen. Not one of them said "Burn a CD." I clicked on the "Help" icon. It said nothing about burning a CD. So I typed "burn a CD" into the box next to "Search." One of the options was, "Copy files and folders to a CD" and "Tips for writing CDs." Nothing about burning. "Are copying, writing, and burning the same thing?" I wondered. I clicked on "Copy. . . ." Immediately, a split screen popped up listing (in very small print I might add) six sequential directions and four bulleted notes. I stared at the words. I knew they were English because I had seen all of them separately many times before. Linked together, however, they made no sense. I stared at them, willing my head to turn them into something meaningful. They mocked me. *If the files are located in My Pictures, under Picture Tasks, click Copy to CD or Copy all items to CD, and then skip to step 5.* I wanted to skip town. I reached for the phone and dialed my son's number. I said, "Brad, I have to burn a CD. Will this involve fire?" I had awakened him and he muttered, "Mom, you don't deserve to own a computer. . . ."

Donna ultimately learned to do it, but only when her son, now awake and apologetic, walked her through it step-by-step. As a matter of fact, she found that it's quite an easy process. So easy, her friend Sandy tells her, that her three-year-old granddaughter does it without needing to be shown how!

Donna needed someone to show her another way. She was working in an area that was foreign to her. Her word identification skills weren't enough: she couldn't make meaning. To many students, the course textbook is like this. They see words they recognize, or maybe not, but the meaning just won't come. Like Donna, they need someone to show them another way.

All Students Need Good Teaching

We know that good teaching is critical for those who struggle. But we contend that good teaching is good for everyone. We both remember Mickey, a stellar scholar and well-rounded young man. He applied only to the most selective universities and was accepted by all of them. When we saw him on a break from his Ivy League university, we asked him how things were going, certain that he was sailing through his freshman year with no problems. What he said shocked us. "I'm studying six to ten hours a day and I'm number twenty out of twenty-five in all my classes." How could this be? He was a brilliant student! But he had entered another realm, a rarefied atmosphere where everyone was as academically gifted as he was.

Good teaching attends to both *content* and *process*. Mickey had mastered the content of his K–12 courses, by what means we do not know. He was able to "get it," most often without anyone teaching him *how* to "get it." Suddenly he was faced with studies more difficult than he had ever known. He lacked a conscious knowledge of the *processes* of learning. He had a problem—how to get to the content when the learning was not coming easily or quickly. Struggling students face this problem every day. The gap between content and process has caught up with them. We need to model and make transparent the processes for learning for *all* students so that *whenever* they begin to struggle, they have the tools they need to keep moving forward. We need to teach *all* students well.

Regardless of the subject we teach, we want our students to get our course content. Beyond that, however, we believe that we all have a higher goal. Of course we need to prepare them to be able read in a broad sense (from print text, visuals, digital text, the world) and compose texts (written, drawn, oral, digital) to get through our courses and our schools. But, as a bigger mission, we need to prepare them for life beyond our doors, well into adulthood, so that they are equipped with strategies for accomplishing whatever they choose. For Mickey, it was an Ivy League education. For others, it might be to learn procedures and communicate successfully on the job site, in the community, and as a citizen. For all, it is much more than showing progress on a standardized test. Good teaching of both content and process is an issue we can ill afford to ignore. It is the right of all learners.

Instruction Needs Scaffolding

When Philadelphia work crews started to clean the statue of William Penn atop City Hall, they first installed scaffolding. They took time to build the scaffold from the roof, up around the statue's base, the legs, the torso, and finally the head and the hat. Only then did the real cleaning begin. His hat began to sparkle, then his head. At that point, the workers dismantled the top part of the scaffold. Week after week, Penn's neck, shoulders, torso, legs, and feet began to shine, sections of the scaffold coming down when they were no longer needed. Finally, the entire statue gleamed in the late afternoon sun, all traces of scaffolding removed.

Teaching students is a lot like cleaning William Penn. We need to take the time to build scaffolds for students so they can "reach" the high points we want them to attain. When the scaffold is no longer needed, we take it down, piece by piece.

Scaffolding is one way that teachers help organize information so that our students' brains can make sense of it. In our everyday lives, how many of us just stuff things into file cabinets and then become totally frustrated when we have to dig through the clutter to find what we need? Self-help books and TV shows have emerged in response to this situation, with professional organizers sharing their tips for conquering our files, closets, and spare rooms. This is what we need to do for our students. We need to help them stay organized—not just their notebooks and lockers but their brains too. Yes, we know that they multitask, listening to music, texting their friends, watching TV, and doing their homework, perhaps none of it well. But how we do help them prioritize the clutter? How do we make sure that important information is filed away in their permanent memories? Our lectures, our reading assignments, and our note taking all make more sense if we can supply a scaffold, an organizing framework.

Scaffolds can take many forms. Sometimes they appear in words, other times in demonstrations; still other times they are multisensory. We build them to provide the support students need at a particular time and take them down when that support is no longer needed.

The Before, During, and After of Lessons Need to Be Rethought

As teachers, we are always caught in a time crunch; we just want to get on with it. Hurry our students into the lesson, spew out the content, and tie up loose ends before the bell rings. Over many years, however, we've learned that we get a bigger payoff in student learning if we take the time to think of lessons in three important phases: before, during, and after.

Before. This is our opportunity to grab them, to get them to start making connections between where they are and what's coming. It's the bridge between wherever their minds have been—social chatting, last period's test, what's on the lunch menu—and where we want their minds to be. More than just an attention grabber (although this is important), it's the place where we access students' prior knowledge and ask them to hypothesize and predict what new content might follow. It's also when we equip them with any strategies they will need to process the lecture, text, video, or demonstration we're presenting.

Although adding another phase to lesson design in order to make the rest of the lesson faster and more efficient may sound counterintuitive, we've found it to be true. Taking time to establish the "hook" to lure students into a lesson, to access their prior knowledge, to get them to hypothesize and predict, and to preteach any necessary strategies pays off. It allows us to cover more content, more deeply. The reason? We have to spend less time stopping and reteaching during and after the lesson because students are involved and equipped from the start.

John, the science teacher, walked into the senior chemistry class and said, "Ladies, today I'm going to tell you about the test of true love. And gentlemen, you listen up, too, because I want you to know that I'm telling the ladies about this." Smiling at their sudden attention, he continued, "Now, I know you're going to be meeting the true love of your life in the foreseeable future. One day, he'll get down on one knee, open a jewel box containing a beautiful diamond ring, and ask for your hand in marriage. Here comes the test of true love. Before you say yes, take the ring and go to the closest window. Take the stone and rub it over the glass. If it scratches the glass, say yes, because it's a real diamond representing true love. If it doesn't, hand it right back to him and say an emphatic no. You see, a diamond is the hardest mineral. It not only scratches glass, it's used in drills to cut through the hardest of substances." The class was riled. Both genders objected. "Wait a minute—you can't say that love is equal to a concrete object!" "What if he doesn't have any money!" "Not fair!" "Cruel!" John demurred. "Okay, okay. So it's bad advice, but now that I have your attention, let me show you what's really true." He raised a shade that had been hiding a chart depicting the hardness scale from talc to diamond, and the class was up and running.

John knew something important about teaching. He knew he had to start where the students were, then build a bridge to where he wanted them to be. It was spring. Love, prom dates, and graduation into a future life were in the air these seniors breathed. Somehow he needed to get them excited about learning the hardness scale. So he connected the two as an invitation to his lesson.

During. This is the body of a lesson, where we ask students to read, listen to, or view the content that we care so much about. We need to guide this interaction—as much or as little as the students need in order to learn successfully. This act of *guiding* them is something that is easy to ignore, but for students who struggle, it is imperative. For those who, like Mickey, don't struggle *yet*, this guidance models various ways of thinking about and understanding oral, written, or viewed texts—ways of thinking that will become important to them at some point in their learning lives. Guidance for students who need more help than those like Mickey might include graphic organizers, reading guides, guided note-taking schemes, or verbal cueing and be interspersed with sketches, musical cues, physical props, or movement.

John gathered his students around his huge lab desk on which were various minerals that he identified and characterized before demonstrating what each could do. As the students watched and listened, they took notes on a simple four-column form he had them make by folding a notebook page into four columns and labeling them "Mineral," "Best Guess," "Characteristics," and "Results." Combined with minimal verbal cueing—"Take a moment to notice the characteristics," "Jot your comments about the results"—this little bit of guidance let them know what the key learning areas were.

After. We know this part of the lesson well. It's where we sum up and lead students in what we call the 4Cs: checking, confirming, changing, and clarifying. It's the jumping-off place for future explorations that extend and enrich what we've taught. In many cases, it's done in a final burst of breath as we try to beat the clock before the bell rings. It can also be a time of great frustration if we find that students haven't gotten it, have misinterpreted it, or just don't care. The better we do in the before stage, the better students do in the during and after stages.

With just a couple of minutes left in the period, John said, "Okay. Tell me something you learned today." Like an orchestra conductor with a baton, he pointed to individual students. His students were accustomed to having him do this and quickly scanned their notes so they would be ready with a response.

This snapshot of John's chemistry class took place over forty years ago. It was the product of a good teacher's intuition. He was not following a mandate, nor was he glomming onto the latest idea du jour. An official before, during, and after lesson design format wasn't researched and codified for another two decades (Lytle and Botel 1988); yet here was a teacher who knew that if he couldn't reach them, he couldn't teach them. He took his cues from students' needs and his sense of what would work well with them. As we reflect on the lessons of our distant past, the ones we remember decades later are those in which a teacher took the time to set us up for success. John is joined by Ken, the social studies teacher who asked students to read book reviews and identify their features before writing them, and Liz, the physical education teacher who had a gymnast model a good routine before breaking it down into its step-by-step parts, and many others. Good teaching is good teaching. Always has been, always will be.

Teachers Need to Do Whatever It Takes

Roberta dresses up in a referee's uniform when she holds a "Super Bowl of Science" as a midyear review in her seventh-grade classes. She enters the classroom bouncing a basketball on the day she's teaching angle of incidence and angle of reflection. To start a unit on body systems, she wears an apron with outlines of body organs and announces that the next topic is "guts."

Donna sings to her university seniors, peppers her teaching with cartoons, and keeps a prop box close at hand for impromptu dramatizations.

On any given day in our classes, students may be sketching their way to understanding. Primary source material and the Internet take their place beside, and sometimes instead of, textbooks.

A peek into our classrooms might show students listening to a lecture, talking in pairs, working in small groups, or doing an activity as a class.

Sometimes we look silly. Sometimes learning comes in a gush of laughter. Most of the time it looks quite different from the schoolmarm presiding over rows of silent children. As Roberta tells her students, "My job is to teach you, not to trick you." Our job is to teach, to do whatever it takes to get students to learn.

Teaching is more than pouring information into sometimes unthirsty minds, but it goes far beyond mere showmanship. If we are the only ones thinking, then our brains are growing, not our students'. Our job is to design lessons that grab them, lure them in, and engage them actively, because it isn't about *us*. It's about *them* and *their* learning. Beyond that, little else matters.

Teachers Need to Learn from Students

Our classrooms are rich research fields, with opportunities for us to study teaching and learning every day. All we have to do is open our eyes and ears, ask questions, and listen to what our students tell us. For example, fourteen-year-old Antonio started the year by handing in assignments and quizzes that would be judged as poor for a third grader. His garbled writing made it difficult to tell whether he understood the science content. Watching him in class, however, Roberta noticed that he raised his hand often, eagerly taking part in discussions and using very sophisticated vocabulary. His answers were spot on. She pulled him aside after class and talked to him. He told her that he *knows* it but just can't write it down, that he needs to hear it to understand it. She began letting him dictate his answers on assignments and quizzes and found that his science knowledge had quite a lot of depth. The dictation also gave him a text of his own words to read and reread, thereby helping him improve his reading.

The simple question "What's going on?" opens immense windows into our students' minds. "What's working?" and "What's not working?" give us insight into how they learn. "How can I help you?" leads to revised lesson procedures and assignments tailored to their needs. Asking them, verbally or in writing, to monitor their learning is a small investment of our energy and time that has a big payoff in directing our teaching.

■ Read On . . .

The field of education has been blessed with three decades of research about differences in how people learn and how teachers can meet these varied needs. Research in learning styles, multiple intelligences, working with English language learners, brain function, and more is reflected in the activities we present in this book. There is no magic pill or fairy dust to sprinkle to help students who struggle. There is only good teaching that incorporates the best from many eras of educational innovation. We have spent our careers listening, reflecting, and pulling together a compendium of lessons that work for us. We are happy to share them with you. We each bring our background of almost forty years in teaching—Roberta in science and Donna in literacy—to the writing of this book.

Yet we know that every school year brings a new start, with new students and new challenges. Although being a teacher is challenging, it is a noble calling. Seeing the light in a struggling student's eyes when he says, "I got it!" makes us realize why we chose this profession. The strategies we've included in this book are designed to help students read text material more effectively, crack vocabulary, write to enhance their reading, learn through many channels, and use their love of technology so that they can better learn and understand the content and so that their eyes light up with the joy of understanding something new. We offer them to you, not as recipes in a cookbook, but as things to try out, tweak, and adapt to your grade and subject area. Make them your own. *All* students need good teachers. Because you have picked up this book, we suspect that you are one of them. We hope you find these strategies useful and that they inspire you to create more of your own.

CHAPTER

Demystifying Reading:
Helping Every Reader Tackle Texts

At the end of each school year, Roberta asks her middle school science students to evaluate their reading growth. In her most recent survey, 96 percent of her students felt that they were better in science reading than in previous years, with 4 percent rating their reading the same. Comments like these are music to her ears:

- I think I do read better in science because I learned to break apart a paragraph or passage to understand it better.

- Now I think I pay attention more to what I read.

- I think that I read better now in science than I first did because of the reading guides mainly. The color-coding vocabulary helped a lot too.

Roberta teaches science, not English/language arts. As a teacher of both content and process, though, she believes that they go hand in hand. Her students understand her content better when she attends to their processes of learning as well. Regardless of the subject you teach, this combination of content and process will yield big results.

■ We Are All Readers—The Teacher, Too

Roberta is a reader and her students know it. From the beginning, talk about books and "readerly" behavior permeates her classroom. She confronts the elephant in the room by asking how many of them like to read science books. She rarely sees more than a couple of hands in the air. She asks why they don't. Timidly at first, then more animatedly when they see that it's okay to be honest, they talk about big words, too much information, and ideas that are hard to understand. A few brave souls flatly state that it just isn't interesting to them.

"It's okay to say it," Roberta concurs, "science books can be very boring." She reassures them that she's not offended by their honesty and that every reader finds certain subjects to be more interesting and easier to read. She tells them part of her job is to help them tackle science texts by sharing strategies that she has found to be successful.

Our students may know very few adults who are readers. Mandatory public education gives us a captive audience from kindergarten through twelfth grade. In that time, we of course want to teach them content. But we have an even greater opportunity. We can be among the few adults with whom our students talk about books—about being a reader.

We need to share our literacy experiences with our students, talking about how we experience reading. What's difficult, pleasurable, triumphant? Let's make it public. Carry around that novel you're reading. Have a newspaper on your desk. Say things like, "Did you see the article in today's paper?" and "I read so late last night I'm really tired today. It was one of those books that you just can't put down." Pave the way for honest talk about what it is to be a reader in today's world.

Understanding Reading

Demystifying reading is good for everyone. Beginning in early elementary school, students have heard important messages about being a good reader, but it is ever so important that they see that the teachers of all their subjects understand, value, and enjoy reading as well. They need to know that their content-area teachers have the same knowledge and expectations regarding literacy as their English teachers do and the same willingness to help students apply what they already know about reading to a new subject or grade level.

Rating Reading Tasks

Over the years, Donna has worked with many students in reading and study skills classes. Most of them regard themselves as poor readers, and many say they were tutored at some point during their schooling. Donna always asks these students to plot the texts they read along a simple arrow from easiest to hardest. She shares her own first.

Their first shock is that a professor with a Ph.D. encounters things that are difficult to read! Their second is that computer-related texts, even the help screen, are hard for her. Next, they draw their own arrows and plot the texts they encounter. The discussion that follows is rich, as they compare and contrast one another's lists. They marvel at how something that is difficult for them is on a classmate's easy list and vice versa. Techno-savvy as their generation is, they

Donna Topping's Reading Task Rating

Easiest   Hardest

→

most novels	teaching books	science texts	computer books
recipes	history books	directions	computer help screen
phone book	plays	legal documents	statistics
most magazines	poetry		
road signs	maps		

good-naturedly tease Donna when they discover that many of them have listed computer texts on the easy side.

Her point is this: There is no such thing as a universally good or universally poor reader. Every reader finds some things easy to read and some things more difficult. What makes one a successful reader is recognizing when a text is challenging and knowing what to do about it. When students rate their reading in each of their classes, they realize where they stand and what they need to do in order to read the material successfully.

■ When Reading Isn't Working

To repeat, it's not that some readers are simply good at reading; it's that successful readers know what to do when they get into trouble. Good readers recognize when something is making sense and when it's not, and they use fix-up strategies to repair what is not working for them. They might use any combination of the following (Topping and McManus 2002, 25):

- Slow down or stop.

- Reread.

- Read on to find out whether the information you need is forthcoming.

- Connect the information in the text to something you already know. (Use your prior knowledge.)

- Predict or hypothesize.

- Visualize a picture in your head.

- Use in-text aids (pictures, headings, titles, graphs).

- Identify the pattern (cause/effect, sequence, a list, compare/contrast, description, problem-solution).

- Identify the controlling idea.

- Use key words and signal words to help discover meaning (*first, next, in summary*).

- Chunk long wordy parts into fewer words.

- Paraphrase.

- Summarize.

- Self-question.

- Talk with someone.

- Write:

  - Underline/highlight.

  - Jot notes in the margin.

  - Say it in your own words.

- Use a decoding strategy to figure out an unknown word:

  - Read to the end of the sentence (context).

  - Try the first few sounds (phonics).

  - Break the word apart (structure).

  - Look it up (dictionary or glossary).

  - Ask for help.

As Donna talks students through these fix-up strategies, she shares how she uses these in her own reading. She describes reading long and rambling passages in her graduate work and not being able to remember the beginning of the sentence by the time she finally reached the period. When they nod in recognition, she describes how she had to *chunk* the run-on sentence, finding the simple subject, verb, and object to get the gist. They laugh when she describes how she has to *reread* computer texts, often out loud—really loud—to help her cope. They roar when she tells them that she has her son-in-law, the technology education teacher, on speed-dial because *talking with someone* is her most-used computer text fix-up. (She has stopped asking her son, who doesn't think she deserves to own a computer.) She asks them to share their experiences. It's always an aha moment when they realize that the very behavior they had regarded as insufficient (*I had to read that three times to get it*) is a sign of strength.

Hearing a teacher say that it's not only *okay* to use these strategies but that she uses them too makes a world of difference. A chart of fix-up strategies should be posted in every classroom, and students should have a copy of the list in their notebook or on bookmarks so they can refer to them as needed. The strategies are not only permissible, they are *necessary*.

The SQ3R Plan

Roberta lays the groundwork by showing students that conversation about books and reading is welcome in her classroom. Then she presents a specific game plan for tackling informational text. Her students have admitted they don't like to read science books. "So what *do* you like to read?" Roberta asks, genuinely interested. They tell her about their tastes in authors and genres, and she shares hers. She's always amazed at how much they enjoy talking about books, and she finds it difficult to stop them. Using this conversation as a segue, she points to a bulletin board on which she has displayed the SQ3R study plan—survey, question, read, recite, review (Robinson 1970):

- *Survey*. Read the title, headings, and subheadings. Look at the pictures, charts, and graphs. Read the opening section and the closing section. Look at the summary section and the checkup questions.

- *Question*. Think about the things you just perused. Turn each of them into questions. For example, if the title is "Anticipating War," your question might be "How were they anticipating war?" If the heading is "Disputes over Territories," your question might be, "What were the disputes about?" If a picture shows people holding each other and screaming, your question might be "Why are they so upset?"

- *Read*. With these questions in mind, begin reading.

- *Recite*. When you've finished reading, return to the questions you asked. Answer them. You may need to reread to clarify any confusion.

- *Review*. Go back and review the answers to previous questions you posed in earlier chapters. Add this new layer of knowledge to it. Keep doing this and you will find that you will be up-to-date when the test rolls around!

SQ3R and study plans like it have been around for a long time, but Roberta ties it to students' prior knowledge. She asks her class how they choose books to read for pleasure and links their responses about browsing—looking at the front and back cover, scanning pages, and so on—to the concept of *survey*. She asks them what things they wonder about as they consider a book, and compares their curiosities about the genre, characters, and action to the *question* phase. She likens going back to make sure which character said what to *rereading* and revisiting the previous chapter to find their place when they pick the book up again to *reviewing*. She concludes by telling them that they have already been doing SQ3R for years. Now they just need to introduce this old friend to their science text. The conversation is chatty and reassuring. They know that Roberta intends to help them succeed.

Craig, a secondary teacher, sets the components of SQ3R to a beat for his urban students. Bringing the plan into the twenty-first century, he leads them into rapping and rhyming their way to understanding:

SQ3R

Hey there, students, this chapter is new.
Some of you are happy and some are so blue.

Look at captions, photos, 'n titles for what they say.
We'll look at all of the info and call it **survey**.

Now activate your brain to develop a **question**.
Are you still having problems or do you need a suggestion?

Your learning's now driven; you're sure to succeed.
So, back to the book; it's now time to **read.**

The work you've done makes you want to **recite**.
You're feeling so proud, assured, and bright.

Finally, we have reached the time to **review**.
Look at the question and answer. How did you do?

When you come to new info, just **SQ3R.**
Then, after the test, you'll be the star.

Craig S. Bradley

The Skim Sandwich

Having little knowledge about a particular subject can make informational texts difficult to read. Reading something that's familiar, our eyes trip lightly across the text, our minds filling in any blanks. When we don't know much about a topic, though, there is not much there with which our minds can connect. The "skim sandwich" (see Figure 2.1) is a useful technique readers can use throughout their lives.

The procedure is simple. After surveying a text to get your bearings, read the first paragraph in its entirety. Then, read the first line of each subsequent paragraph in the text. Finally, read the last paragraph in its entirety. It's amazing what happens. You gain prior knowledge! Not enough, of course, to bypass a careful reading or to take a test, but enough to place you ahead of where you were before you began. Some prior knowledge before you begin reading is better than none, and the skim sandwich provides it. This strategy is also useful when you need to review a text, perhaps before class begins, to remind you of what you read carefully before, in case there's a pop quiz!

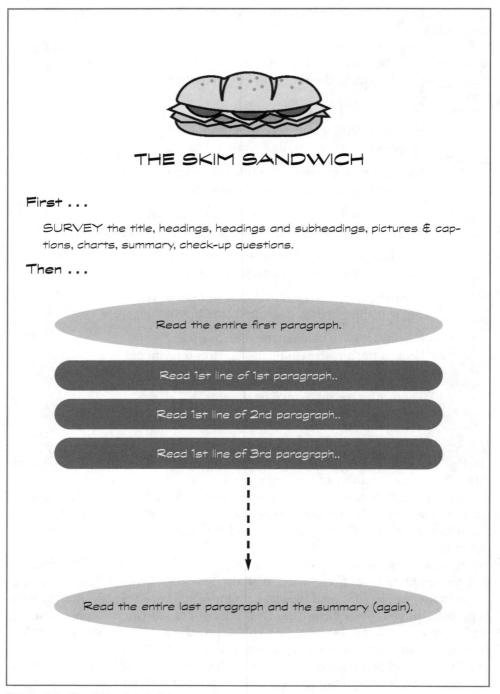

Figure 2.1. The Skim Sandwich

Differentiating Strategies

Roberta is familiar with the curriculum found in prior grades, so she is able to offer pointers for connecting new information to what students have learned earlier. She alerts top readers, who often want to speed through a reading selection, to the places where they will find the newest information and cautions them to slow down there. She spends extra time with struggling readers, pointing out the arrangement of the text, the headings, new vocabulary, and text organization to facilitate their reading and understanding.

The Importance of Modeling and Repetition

Simply introducing a strategy such as SQ3R or the skim sandwich isn't enough. Modeling it and supporting students as they tackle subsequent text assignments must follow throughout the year.

Go through new sections of text together, generating thinking and discussion about the topic *before* students read so that they are able to access prior knowledge. Show how consciously acknowledging what you already know makes it easier to integrate the new to the known.

So often we emphasize the *after* reading stage only and become frustrated by the results. Taking the time to focus on *before* reading strategies in study plans such as SQ3R and skim sandwich pay off in increased comprehension for everyone.

■ Navigating Informational Text

Informational texts are structured differently in ways that go beyond the titles and paragraphs of their literary counterparts. Any reader benefits from breaking down informational text into parts—front matter, middle matter, and end matter—and exploring what information each contains.

Front matter includes important introductory material such as copyright, table of contents, preface, dedication, and acknowledgments, all things that situate the author and text in time and place. The table of contents might be annotated or outlined to show precisely what information is found in each chapter.

Chapters constitute the heart of the text, or the *middle matter*. Within the chapters, authors and editors include a variety of *salience devices*, things such as font type, headings and subheadings, side notes and endnotes, summary and checkup sections, pictures and captions, charts, diagrams, and maps. These features augment the text to make it clearer, or more *salient.*

A text's *end matter* offers the reader assorted references, such as glossary, index, works cited/bibliography, and appendixes. These sections provide a great deal of information that students often skip unless someone points them out. So that's exactly what we should do.

Student _Mark_   Section _S2_

SURVEYING YOUR TEXTBOOK

BOOK PUBLISHING

1. What is the book's title?
   Cells, Heredity, + classification

2. When was this book written? _2002_

3. How can it make a difference if this book was written or revised recently?
   Science info changes

TABLE OF CONTENTS

4. How many chapters are in this book? _7_

5. Examine the following sections found in the Table of Contents. Next, name the activity that goes with our current unit of study (Microscopes and Cells).

FEATURE IN TABLE OF CONTENTS	ACTIVITY FOR THIS UNIT
Chapter Labs	_Cells alive_
Connections	_Cellular ID Cards_
Mathematics	_Cell Multiplication_
Appendix	a. _Scientific Method_
	b. _Using the microscope_

Figure 2.2. Surveying Your Textbook

CHAPTER ONE: Cells: Basic Units of Life

6. Looking at page 2, how many sections are in this chapter? __3__

7. Four other features are listed in this margin. Name them.

    a. _Chapter labs_

    b. _Chapter review_

    c. _Feature articles_

    d. _Lab book_

8. In this chapter, each section is divided in to subsections. The headings for the subsections are written in _Green_ ink.

9. Does Chapter 1 contain the following? (Answer yes or no.)

    _No_ maps   _Yes_ photographs   _Yes_ charts

    Yes section reviews _Yes_ lab work   _Yes_ vocabulary lists

    _No_ graphs   _Yes_ health info   _Yes_ chemistry connections

BACK OF BOOK

10. Check out page 206. What kind of lens is found in the eyepiece?
    Ocular

11. On which pages will you find the glossary? _p. 208-210_

12. In the glossary, what does the number found behind each word mean?
    This is the page where you can find the Word

13. The index is found on pages _211-214_.

14. Name one scientist listed in the index.
    Robert Hooke

15. What do the boldface numbers in the index mean?
    A picture of it is found on that page

Figure 2.2. Continued

Textbook Survey

When Roberta passes out her textbook, she accompanies it with a survey (see Figure 2.2) that walks students through the entire book. Their past experience with science has come primarily through science kits and hands-on exploration, and her course is their first encounter with a science textbook. She begins by calling their attention to information critical in a scientific text—the date of publication. With scientific knowledge changing at an exponential rate, a difference of even a few years makes a big difference.

Then she has students scan the table of contents and notice how it is laid out. After that, she has them examine a typical chapter. She asks them to identify what salience devices are included and consider how they work.

Finally, she refers students to the end matter, asking them to identify information in the appendix, glossary, and index. From the outset, Roberta's students see the text as a rich resource, not just assigned paragraphs for them to read while ignoring everything else.

Creating Textbook Experts

Vary the textbook tour by having students form groups to investigate the textbook's front, middle, and end matter. Have them count off by threes, with 1s focusing on front matter, 2s on middle matter, and 3s on end matter. All the students with the same number meet, note the features in their section of the text, and prepare to report their findings. After this, have them break into triads, each consisting of a 1, a 2, and a 3, to share what they've learned. This group format enables weaker readers not only to benefit from hearing what stronger readers note about their section, but also to be able to shine when they share their "expertise" in the final triads. Everyone wins.

Scavenger Hunts and Other Games People Play

Develop a list of items for students to locate in the front, middle, and end matter of the course text and turn it into a scavenger hunt. *In which chapter will you learn about the Great Depression? In what year was the text published? What does blue print indicate? How many charts are in Chapter 3? On what pages will you find information about Abraham Lincoln? In which appendix will you find a map of the United States?* Teams of four students can compete to see who can find the answers in the shortest time.

Other games commonly played in classrooms, such as Jeopardy (*I'll take front matter for 200 points, please*) and Trash Can Basketball (if your team answers the question correctly, you get a chance to toss the wadded-up paper "ball" into the trash can for two points), can easily be adapted to surveying texts. Playing on teams invites all students into learning.

The time invested in text surveys is worthwhile. Going through the book close-up makes tacking the subject matter less intimidating, especially for those who typically approach reading school texts with trepidation.

QAR Grows Up

Roberta's text survey also introduces the icons she uses to guide students' reading throughout the year. The *book* next to a question or instruction signals that the answer is right there in the text. The *magnifying glass* tells them that the answer is there, but they will have to search a bit, perhaps combining information from different parts of the chapter in order to find it. The *lightbulb* lets them know that they will have to combine what they read in the text with their own thoughts in order to making meaning.

This kind of cueing is very much like question-answer relationships (QAR) (Raphael 1982). In QAR, teachers take the mystery out of question-answer relationships by overtly teaching the kind of thinking involved. A *right there* question is one whose answer is right there in the text. A *think-and-search* question requires more searching within the text. *Author and me* and *on my own* questions require the reader to combine what is in the text with their own thoughts. Many of Roberta's students have been taught the QAR terminology in their elementary school reading classes. Therein lies the rub: "QAR is for babies and we're grown up!" "QAR is for reading and this is science!" So these terms never cross Roberta's lips. Instead, she plays on their sophisticated knowledge of technology and uses icons to indicate the same thing.

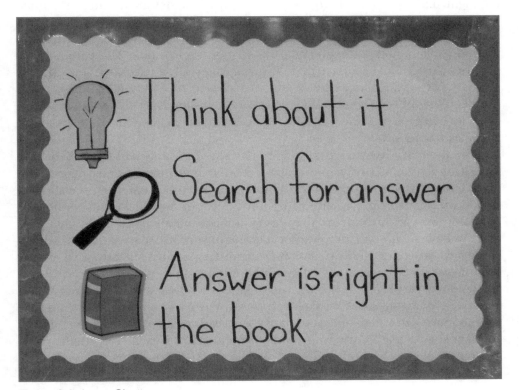

Figure 2.3. Icons Chart

A chart (see Figure 2.3) containing these icons and their meanings hangs in Roberta's room, reminding her students of their purpose. The icons let students know how they should tackle a question. *Should I find it easily in the paragraph? Is the answer somewhere in the text and I should be looking for it? Since I have to think of this answer on my own, what clues does the book give me?* The icons also let students know Roberta's expectations: she offers more help for lightbulb and magnifying glass questions but expects students to be able to find the answers to questions with the book icons. Students quickly learn that Roberta has confidence in them, that they can find the answers on their own! (Readers with significant learning disabilities require more help.)

These icons appear as long as students need them, and are faded out when they are no longer necessary. Advanced and proficient readers generally do not need them beyond the first half of the year; basic and below-basic readers sometimes use them throughout the entire year.

■ Talking to—and Back to—Text

Annotating Text

Successful readers talk back to the texts they read. They annotate, underline, highlight, and write in the margins, particularly when they are dealing with information that is dense or unfamiliar. They note important ideas and key facts. They jot questions and comments in the margins. They place stars beside some information, exclamation points and question marks next to others. This commentary provides a road map of sorts to their thinking when they go back to reread. Unfortunately, because textbooks are expensive and have to be reused, writing in them has been one of the classic taboos of school behavior. Over the years, many an offender has been punished, fined, or at minimum been handed a large eraser for such destructive acts.

How, then, do we teach and guide practice in this important readerly behavior? The invention of sticky notes was a real boon to reading. Because they can be written on, affixed to a page of text, then removed without marring the surface, they have opened up a wealth of opportunities for teaching students how to annotate texts. Unfortunately, they come at a cost, and when the supply dwindles, we have to dip into our own pockets and buy more. We have developed two strategies, *text boxes* and *text brackets*, as an economical substitute when our accounts are overdrawn at the office supply store.

Text boxes (see Figure 2.4) allow you to jot notes to guide your students' transactions with texts and ask for their responses. Their best feature is they are very easy to make. On a blank piece of paper, simply draw a box for each paragraph, chart, or special feature you want students to note. Label each box with the paragraph number or chart title; add any guidance, task, or question that you want; and make a copy for each student.

Textboxes   **Page 57**

NOTES	REACTIONS/QUESTIONS
Unraveling the Mystery Mendel chose to study only one kind of organism—pees	How can a trait skip a generation an then, show up again?
How Do You Like Your Peas? peas were a good choice because! 1) grow quicly, 2) meny Varieties, 3) = male and female parts on the Same plant <u>self pollination</u>	<u>pollination</u>—pollen moves from male to female part of flower <u>fertilization</u> egg and sperm join
FIGURE 2. flowers have male and female parts.	sperm are in the polle
FIGURE 3. <u>pollination</u> happens first, then fertilization. 1) wind 2) animal 3) self.	This is sexual reprodution

Figure 2.4. Text Boxes

Text brackets (see Figure 2.5) are equally simple to make. Fold a piece of paper in half lengthwise, thus creating four columns for brackets (two on the front side, two on the back). With the paper folded, lay it next to the left-hand margin of the first page of text. Draw brackets to indicate each paragraph or figure. Flip the folded paper over to the second column and bracket the paragraphs and figures

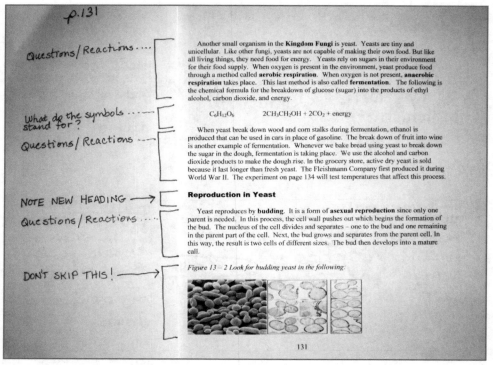

Figure 2.5. Text Brackets with side-coaching comments

for the second page of text. Do the same for the third and fourth page of text, using the two columns on the back of the paper. With either format, the intention is the same—to scaffold students' communication with text.

What gets included on text boxes and brackets? Get inside your readers' heads and think of what would help them the most in any given reading assignment. Here are some possibilities to get you started.

Comprehension monitoring. Have students consciously monitor their comprehension by placing a code next to each paragraph or text feature. Follow up on this after reading by asking about what parts they "got" and didn't "get," what questions they have, and what they found surprising or interesting. Sample codes:

✓ I get it.

❓ I don't get it or I have a question.

❗ This surprised me or this was interesting.

Topic sentences or main idea statements. Alert students to the topic sentence or main idea statement by writing it in the box or next to the bracket. You can vary this by using symbols to indicate the approximate place in the paragraph where they will find this sentence or statement:

▽   beginning of paragraph

△   end of paragraph

◇   middle of paragraph

⧖   double statement, at beginning and end of paragraph

○   an unstated topic or main idea statement

Key vocabulary. Point out key vocabulary by writing the words next to the paragraphs in which they occur, including definitions if necessary. You can vary this by listing the words and having students define them in their own words, using context, after reading the paragraph or text feature.

Reading rate. Successful readers vary their reading rate according to the characteristics of the text material. Students often just plod through, reading everything at the same pace. You can scaffold the rate with which they proceed by adding clip art icons in the boxes or next to the brackets for each section of text.

Sample icons:

   Read at a normal rate.

   Slow down; read carefully.

   Stop and think about this.

   Skim; read quickly.

Side-coaching. Look at your text with new eyes. If you could sit next to each of your students, what would you say about it as they read? Write these things in the boxes or next to the brackets. Side-coaching can be very helpful when your text is not as thorough or clear as it might be. Following are some sample comments.

This is important.

This will be on the test.

This part is confusing, and we'll talk more about this in class.

A fact not included here is . . . .

This explains why . . . .

Think about how you would feel if . . . .

You may need to read this paragraph twice.

Don't skip this chart.

Notice the new heading.

Why do you think they didn't . . . ?

Sticking Points

Reserve your office supply budget for purchasing narrow (about a half-inch wide) sticky notes. Limit each student to a few of them (five or so, depending on the passage in the text). Tell them that they should affix a sticky note to each major point they feel is most important to have "stick" in their minds. Because the number is limited, they may have to remove notes and reconsider points that they mark, so that the major ideas ultimately earn the sticky notes. The rereading and reconsideration involved in this activity are an excellent exercise in differentiating main ideas from details, a readerly behavior that is central to success. It also lays the groundwork for ultimately being able to highlight text instead of simply coloring the page yellow with a highlighter, unable to distinguish gradations of importance.

What happens to these sticking points, once identified? Students can present and defend their choices in small groups, ultimately reporting their consensus to the whole class. They can list them in their notes or turn them into a tersely written summary paragraph. The thinking, talking, and writing involved with this simple technique pay big dividends in helping all students learn and retain important information.

■ The Guide on the Side

Much like side-coaching, reading guides prompt students through a series of directions, notations, and responses. They allow you to sit beside each of your students as he or she reads, pointing out what is important in the text and how to read it successfully. One-to-one instruction? Not literally, but as close as content teachers can get with class sizes hovering around thirty.

We have used reading guides with all kinds of texts—textbooks, primary source material, magazine articles, Internet sources—and commercially prepared guides proliferate. As with many things in education, reading guides can take on a life of their own, good ideas that "everyone's doing." We have seen—and created—really good ones and really bad ones. We suggest you develop or select them with a discriminating eye. Begin by putting yourself inside your students' heads and asking:

- Is there anything about the structure of the text that they need to note?

- What access features might they notice or not notice?

- What information might they understand or not understand?

- What aspects might they interpret correctly or incorrectly?

- What are the key points that, if they do not grasp, will be a critical loss to their understanding?

- At what rate(s) should students read this text?

The type of guide depends on your *purpose*. Is it to:

- introduce the topic?

- extend students' understanding?

- help students apply knowledge?

- guide students in forming an opinion?

- help students draw conclusions?

- allow students to practice test-taking skills?

Your purpose clues you in about how a guide should be structured.

Introducing Material

When Roberta is using a text to introduce information, she gives the page number, even the paragraph number, where the information is located. To those who say, "But that's pointing out the answers!" she replies, "That's right. That's my job." Her texts are dense with scientific information, and her novice scientists quickly become overwhelmed. They get caught up in minute details and facts, unable to distinguish more important from less important information. Roberta is the "senior scientist." Early in a unit, they need her close hand-holding, the direction of an expert to guide their novice explorations.

Figure 2.6 is an introductory reading guide. Roberta includes a *before* stage, in which she asks students to recall their prior knowledge by examining the first three text headings and listing things they know. Using the headings found in the

Cytologist _____ Section _____

Chapter 1: CELLS: The Basic Units of Life

ORGANIZATION OF LIFE, pages 4-8

1. **BEFORE** reading, look at the three subsections found on pages 4 and 5. (They are in green ink.) Next, using complete sentences, write three things that you already know about these topics.

   a. _____

   b. _____

   c. _____

PARAGRAPH 1, page 4

2. How many cells are in you? _____

CELLS: STARTING OUT SMALL, page 4

Write out TRUE or FALSE as your answer.

   _____ 3. A microscope is needed to see most cells.

   _____ 4. We all began as a single cell.

   _____ 5. The human body contains about 200 different kinds of cells that perform specialized functions or jobs.

TISSUES: CELLS WORKING IN TEAMS, page 5

6. Define *tissue*. _____

   _____

7. Examine Figure 3 and give three examples of cells that make up tissues.

   _____   _____   _____

ORGANS: TEAMS WORKING TOGETHER, page 5

8. Groups of tissues make _____.

Figure 2.6. Introductory Reading Guide (*continues*)

9. Name three organs found in your body.

   _____   _____   _____

10. Name the largest organ in your body. _____

11. FACT: In your lifetime, you will shed almost 40 pounds (18 kilograms) of
    dead skin! Yuck!

ORGAN SYSTEMS: A GREAT COMBINATION, page 6

12. Define organ system. _____

    _____

13. What is the job of your nervous system? _____

    _____

ORGANISMS: INDEPENDENT LIVING, page 7

14. Define organism. _____

15. What does *unicellular* mean? _____

16. How do the cells of unicellular organisms differ from the cells of multi-
    cellular organisms?

    _____

    _____

17. Can your blood cells live outside of your body? _____

THE BIG PICTURE, pages 7 and 8 (Matching: Take a good look—there
are four answers and six questions. Therefore, you will have to use
some answers more than once!)

_____ 18. a desert

_____ 19. the birds, snakes, and squirrels in a forest   a. organism

_____ 20. all of the grasshoppers in a field   b. population

_____ 21. an eagle

_____ 22. soil, rocks, birds, trees, and bugs in a forest   c. community

_____ 23. whales, sharks, and jellyfish in the ocean   d. ecosystem

Figure 2.6. *Continued*

text, she then points them to the page and paragraph where they can find key information. Throughout the guide, she continues to use the icons she introduced during the text survey to let them know the type of reading required. In item 7, she asks for information found in pictures, because she knows that they are likely to skip this nonprint feature. Because she finds that her text overlooks information that students need or would find interesting, she often adds a FACT, as in item 11.

Roberta presents the guide with a brief overview and reminds students to read it all before working with it. After answering any questions, she sets them to work while she circulates. She comes upon one student who is stumped by the before section, insisting that he does not know any facts.

"Cells are verrrrrry . . . ," she prompts.

"Small?" he asks.

"Good, write that sentence down!" He does, then is stumped again, so Roberta offers another prompt. "Name an organ in your body."

He shrugs.

She clutches her middle and says, "What's right here?"

"Fat?" he replies. Not the answer she was looking for! Oops.

He immediately realizes his gaffe, but Roberta reassures him with a laugh. "We had tacos for lunch. Where did your taco go?"

"Oh," he says, "my stomach!"

Working with adolescents is never dull!

Extending Students' Understanding

When students approach a reading task with prior knowledge already established, the guides take on a different look (see Figure 2.7). Although the format is different, Roberta incorporates the same kind of guidance, providing *before* activities, page numbers, and icons.

Before students read, they must use their prior knowledge to hypothesize about fifteen key ideas in the text, rating them as either true or false. Roberta advises students to use SQ3R as they read. This time, she asks them to provide the page number on which they find the information. (When working with students who need extra help, she unobtrusively provides the page number as she circulates.) Once they have found the information, she asks them to confirm or change their true/false prediction and then rewrite false statements to make them true. She lets them know that the underlined words in the statements are the ones central to the truth or falsehood of the statement and that these words should appear in the rewritten statements. (When working with more capable students, she eliminates this underlining.)

Reading Guide   Chapter 1, Section 2, pp. 9-15
The Discovery of CELLS

DIRECTIONS:

1. Before reading this section in your book, read each statement and hypothesize if it's true or false.
2. Use your SQ3R skills to carefully read this section, and list the page number where the information is found.
3. Write whether each statement is true or false.
4. If the statement is false, rewrite it to make it true.

BEFORE Reading: Choose TRUE or FALSE.	STATEMENT (HINT: Pay close attention to the underlined words.)	List the page # on which the information is found.	AFTER Reading: Choose TRUE or FALSE.	If FALSE, rewrite the statement to make it true.
1.	1. Cells were named and discovered by <u>Robert Hooke</u>.			
2.	2. Hooke saw his first cells by looking at the <u>honeycomb in a beehive</u>.			
3.	3. Leeuwenhoek compared the <u>blood cells of various animals</u>.			

Figure 2.7. Reading Guide for Extending Understanding (*continues*)

BEFORE Reading: Choose TRUE or FALSE.	STATEMENT (HINT: Pay close attention to the underlined words.)	List the page # on which the information is found.	AFTER Reading: Choose TRUE or FALSE.	If FALSE, rewrite the statement to make it true.
4.	4. Both Schwann and Schleiden observed that <u>all plants and animals are made of cells.</u>			
5.	5. Virchow determined that all cells <u>come from other cells.</u>			
6.	6. <u>All cells are the same shape and size</u> but have different functions.			
7.	7. The job of the <u>cell wall</u> is to control movement of materials into and out of the cell.			
8.	8. The hereditary material in the cell is <u>DNA, which controls all of the activities of the cell.</u>			
9.	9. Membranes surround <u>all organelles.</u>			

Figure 2.7. *Continues*

BEFORE Reading: Choose TRUE or FALSE.	STATEMENT (HINT: Pay close attention to the underlined words.)	List the page # on which the information is found.	AFTER Reading: Choose TRUE or FALSE.	If FALSE, rewrite the statement to make it true.
10.	10. Cytoplasm is found in <u>all cells</u>.			
11.	11. The cells found in an elephant are <u>larger</u> than those found in a mouse.			
12.	12. In the human body, <u>all cells are alike</u>.			
13.	13. Cells that do not have a nucleus are called <u>prokaryotic cells or bacteria</u>.			
14.	14. Prokaryotic cells are ten times <u>larger</u> than eukaryotic cells.			
15.	15. <u>Both</u> eukaryotic cells and prokaryotic cells contain DNA.			

Figure 2.7. *Continued*

Helping Students Apply Their Knowledge

Near the end of a genetics unit, Roberta addresses cloning, a topic that is not in the textbook. She has developed a guide to an article from *Current Science* to scaffold students' application of both their science and their reading skills (see Figure 2.8). The guide follows her now familiar before, during, and after plan. Before reading, students access their prior knowledge; after reading they apply their learning to a personal question about their family pet. Roberta phases out page and paragraph numbers during the reading. Instead, she calls their attention to a chart, a text feature she knows they might skip, in which four potentially frustrating key terms are beautifully explained. Items 13 through 16 require them to study the chart and select the best definition for each term. Before they read, she alerts them to this new reading guide feature and reminds them of other charts they have examined together previously.

When using a reading guide like this, Roberta adapts the tasks to match students' abilities. Her concern is that they all get the same content, but without becoming overwhelmed by completing the guide. If she is working with a class of predominantly weaker readers or those who have difficulty writing, she requires them to give fewer examples or reasons and offers fewer possible answers to multiple-choice questions. With a class of more able readers and writers, she quietly substitutes questions as she circulates around the room.

Helping Students Form and Support an Opinion

As the genetics unit progresses each year, students always become interested in DNA analysis. They bring their layperson's knowledge of it from watching TV shows and from hearing about it in the news. They become highly opinionated about whether it should be done. Like many adults, they do not want to be confused by the facts! Recognizing an opportunity to show them how to sift through information fairly before forming an opinion, an important life skill, Roberta has prepared a guide to an article titled "History Test" (see Figure 2.9).

Before they read, she gives them ten statements to which they respond either true or false, based on their prior knowledge about DNA. (For students who have reading difficulties, she underlines the critical words in each statement that are central to deciding whether it is true or false.) Then they read the article. After reading, they return to the true/false statements and answer them again based on what they have learned. Finally she asks a series of questions to develop their ability to empathize—to see both sides of an issue before forming an opinion.

Practicing Test-Taking Skills

State tests in reading and science loom large in Roberta's school district, and she and her colleagues want their students to score better in nonfiction reading. Because nonfiction reading strategies come naturally to her, it is easy for Roberta to fold test-taking practice into her reading guides. Periodically, she develops

Genetic Engineer _____ Section _____

Reference: Current Science, 9/10/05, pages 4 and 5

COPY CATS

BEFORE READING: Give two facts that you already know about how Dolly the sheep was cloned in 1996.

a. _____

b. _____

DURING READING

1. Cloning is _____. (Circle the best answer.)

   a. genetic engineering

   b. the manipulation (arranging) of DNA to create identical twins

   c. the creation of genetically engineered organisms

   d. a process that produces twins that are not the same age

   e. all of the above

   f. only a and c

2. How much does it currently cost for a person to have a pet's cells stored by GSC company? _____

3. Why are these cells stored in a freezer?

   a. so that the cells don't get hot and burst

   b. because cells normally die when out of the body

   c. so they don't try to grow

4. _____ True or false? It is legal to work on the cloning of people in the USA.

Figure 2.8. Reading Guide for Applying Knowledge (*continues*)

5. Give three reasons why people do not approve of pet cloning.

 a. _____

 b. _____

 c. _____

6. Calico cats do not necessarily look identical to their twin because ____.

 a. a mutation happened

 b. calico cats are weird

 c. sometimes a gene can be "turned off"

7. Give three reasons why cloned pets can have different personalities.

 a. _____

 b. _____

 c. _____

8. Define temperament (as applied to an animal). _____

 _____

9. _____ True or false? Some cloned animals seem to have the same personalities as their twin.

10. What are two benefits (good results) of cloning pets?

 a. _____

 b. _____

11. Different breeds of dogs are produced by ____.

 a. genetic engineering

 b. cloning

 c. selective breeding

 d. mutations

12. _____ True or false? At this time horses, goats, and dogs have also been cloned.

Figure 2.8. *Continues*

CHART: HOW TO COPY A CAT

13. In Step 2, *enucleated* means to _____.

    a. copy the nucleus in cell division

    b. decrease the number of chromosomes

    c. clone the nucleus of the cell

    d. remove the nucleus from the cell

14. In step 4, *fused* means to _____.

    a. join

    b. split

    c. electrify

    d. clone

15. In Step 5, the best definition of *embryo* is _____.

    a. the cloned animal

    b. the unborn animal

    c. the newborn baby

    d. the fused cells

16. In Step 6, *surrogate* means _____.

    a. cloned mom

    b. cloned baby

    c. egg donor

    d. substitute mom

AFTER READING: If you could, would you clone your family pet? _____Why?

Figure 2.8. *Continued*

guides containing question and answer choices that not only are scientifically appropriate but also mirror the types found on the state tests (items 7 through 13 in Figure 2.10 are examples). She always has her questions vetted by the school's reading specialist, who knows a lot about test formats and is a valuable resource.

Published Versus Personalized Reading Guides

Roberta began one year using a textbook for which she had developed her own reading guides. Halfway through the year, her district received new textbooks that came with publisher-developed reading guides. Pressed for time as she familiarized herself with the new text, she started using the publisher's guides instead of creating her own. But her students asked her to go back to making her own because hers helped them understand the reading better. She has found again and again that if she listens to her students, they will steer her teaching in the right direction every time.

Roberta finds some of the questions and activities in publisher-developed guides are wonderful; others seem to skimp on the reasoning she is looking for. Some fit with her students' needs; others are not a good match. None of them seem to embed the before-during-after structure she likes to use. Taking the best of the published guides and blending them with her own allows her to personalize the guides for particular classes and subjects, adding icons and clip art and always referring to her students as scientists—genetic engineers, cytologists, chemists, microscopists, naturalists, whatever term matches the area of study.

■ Getting the Text into the Class

We wish we could just assign reading and have students go off by themselves and read the text accurately. The reality is quite different. There are times and classes in which the text must be read aloud in order for all students to understand it. How do we do this, fighting off our own bad memories of a teacher droning on and on or the dreaded "round-robin" reading by student after student? Consider these possibilities.

Teacher-Led Reading

In the techniques that follow, the teacher (or other adult) reads the text but varies it in some way so that it doesn't become one long drone.

Thinking aloud. As students follow along in their own books, you read aloud, pausing periodically to tell them what you are thinking, either about the content or your reading process:

> Oh, that's just like what happened in the last chapter.

> So, the forces were hidden from view when the siege took place.

Geneticist _____ Section _____ p. # _____

Current Science, December 14, 2007

    # HISTORY TEST

DIRECTIONS: BEFORE reading the article, read each statement, take a guess and mark it as either true or false in the "before reading" column. AFTER reading, read each statement again and decide if it is true or false and mark it in the "after reading" column. (Reminder—write out TRUE or FALSE.)

BEFORE READING	STATEMENT	AFTER READING
	1. A person has to pay thousands of dollars to have their DNA examined to study ethnic origins.	
	2. Every cell in your body contains DNA.	
	3. Segments of the DNA molecule are called *genes*.	
	4. DNA can be gathered simply by swabbing the inside of your cheek with a Q-tip.	
	5. This type of genetic testing can identify the origins of ALL your ancestors.	
	6. Many believe that this science is flawed (not entirely correct) due to all of the moving around the world that humans have done throughout history.	
	7. Mitochondrial DNA is inherited only from the female parent.	
	8. The sex chromosomes of all woman are both X's.	
	9. A genome is your entire genetic code of DNA.	
	10. Males have both an X and a Y sex chromosome. Their Y chromosome doesn't change much through heredity.	

Figure 2.9. Reading Guide for Forming and Supporting an Opinion (*continues*)

Give reasons why someone WOULD want to have their DNA examined.	Give reasons why someone WOULD NOT want to have their DNA examined.
Do you want to have your DNA examined? Why or why not?	Do you have any more questions about this article?

Figure 2.9. *Continued*

Biologist _____   Section _____

Reference: *Current Science, January 6, 2006, pages 6 and 7*

FADE TO WHITE

Page 6

1. Why are the sands in most deserts brown? _____
   _____

2. Why are the sands in the White Sands National Monument different than most soils in other deserts?
   _____

3. DIRECTIONS: Put the following events in the proper order. Number one has been done for you.

   _____ Brown lizards living in the desert around the lake were hidden from predators by their brown color.

   _____ Rain dissolved the gypsum and carried it down the valley to form a huge lake.

   _____ Wind blew the gypsum out of the lake bed into the surrounding desert.

   __1__ Pounding rain broke down the gypsum rock in the mountains.

   _____ White sand from the lake bed covered the surrounding area.

   _____ The water in the lake evaporated.

   _____ White lizards thrived in the area.

Page 7

4. Why does Ms. Rosenblum collect the snipped-off tails of lizards?

   _____
   _____
   _____

Figure 2.10. Reading Guide for Practicing Test-Taking Skills (*continues*)

5. Describe the mutation that occurred in a few lizards in this area.

_____

_____

_____

6. Natural selection is often described as "survival of the fittest." Why are the white lizards better suited than brown lizards to survive in this desert today?

_____

_____

_____

7. The DNA between the brown lizards and the white lizards living only 19 miles apart

   a. is very different from each other.

   b. has opposite nucleotide bases from each other.

   c. has only one gene that is different.

   d. is exactly the same.

8. How do the scientists know that the two groups of lizards are the same species?

_____

_____

_____

9. What other living thing is most likely to be evolving into a white organism in the White Sands National Monument?

   a. cactus

   b. swans

   c. snakes

   d. butterflies

Figure 2.10. *Continues*

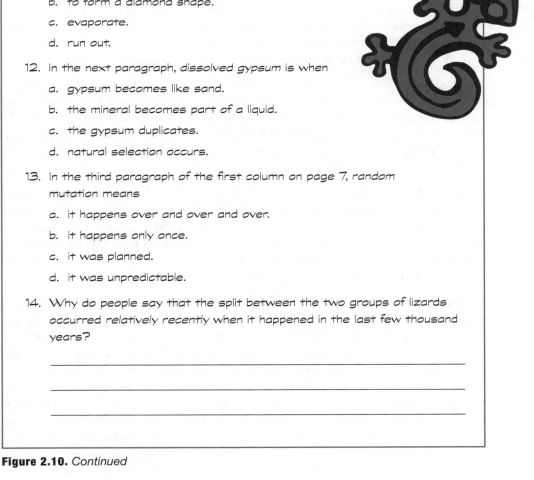

LANGUAGE ARTS CONNECTION

10. In the first paragraph of this article, what does *to lasso* mean?

    a. put in a can

    b. catch with a net

    c. hang

    d. catch with a rope or string

11. In the first paragraph of column 2 on page 6, *crystallizes out of solution* means to

    a. become a solid.

    b. to form a diamond shape.

    c. evaporate.

    d. run out.

12. In the next paragraph, *dissolved gypsum* is when

    a. gypsum becomes like sand.

    b. the mineral becomes part of a liquid.

    c. the gypsum duplicates.

    d. natural selection occurs.

13. In the third paragraph of the first column on page 7, *random mutation* means

    a. it happens over and over and over.

    b. it happens only once.

    c. it was planned.

    d. it was unpredictable.

14. Why do people say that the split between the two groups of lizards occurred *relatively recently* when it happened in the last few thousand years?

    _____

    _____

    _____

Figure 2.10. *Continued*

Huh? Let me read that again!

Here's a footnote; let's see what it says.

As I look at this graph, I'm wondering why. . . .

Guest readers. This takes some advance planning, but you can ask other adults from the school or community to come to your class to read the text aloud. Who do your students admire? The principal? The football coach? The guy who manages the local snack shop? Sometimes just a different timbre, a new voice, will pique students' interest in what the text says. (Make sure you offer the book to your guest readers ahead of time, and suggest that they rehearse!)

Recordings. Some texts come with a recording of a good reader reading it aloud, a welcome support for students who need to hear the text as well as see it. If your text doesn't include this feature, you can make your own recording using whatever technology is available to your students—audiotapes, CDs, or podcasts. Be sure to consult your school's policy regarding recordings, and be aware that you may need permission from the publisher as well. You might share the task of creating a recording with your colleagues, parent volunteers, or senior citizens groups.

Stopping and writing. While students follow along, read the text aloud, stopping at meaningful places (at the end of a paragraph or a short section, for example) and asking students to write what they remember from that portion—key words, thoughts, or questions. Continue like this until the selection is completed. Then ask students to share what they have written and ask questions they have, and clarify any misunderstandings.

The pause that refreshes. While you're reading aloud, students are supposed to be following along in their own books. But what if they are daydreaming or otherwise zoning out? Announce that you are going to read a passage but will pause before key words or phrases. A pause is their signal to read the next word or phrase aloud as a group. (You can draw out the word that precedes your pause to alert them that it's coming: *The process is callllllllled. . . .*)

Trading the teacher role. This technique is based on Manzo's (1969) reciprocal questioning strategy ReQuest. Read the first paragraph of a text aloud while students follow along in their books. Then ask students to close their books while you ask them questions. Read the next paragraph aloud, then close your book. Challenge students to "play teacher" and, with their books open, ask you questions. Continue to alternate the questioner role while you read the rest of the paragraphs in the selection aloud. Initially, students will tend to ask very low-level recall questions, enjoying the chance to trip you up on figures and exact dates. When this happens, model how you look back at the text to clarify small details. When you are the questioner, ask about important ideas that provoke the kind of thinking and comprehension you seek. Students will begin to do the same while having fun "playing teacher."

Choral reading. As the name suggests, you and your students read aloud together as you model and support fluency.

Student-Led Reading

During traditional round-robin reading, students count ahead to see which paragraph will be theirs, quietly rehearse so they will be ready, then collapse in relief (or embarrassment) after they've taken their turn. Little comprehension of the whole text takes place; they take their turn and that's it. In the techniques that follow, students take an active role in reading the text aloud in a safe environment that respects their comfort level and allows them to relate to the text.

Jumping in. Some students want to read aloud; others don't. This technique respects that. After introducing the passage, tell students that you are going to be quiet now, and that someone will jump in and read the first paragraph. When that person finishes, she or he will be quiet and someone else will jump in to read the next, and so on. What if no one jumps in? Someone will! We have used this technique with hundreds of students and someone always jumps in. There will be pauses and silences along the way (providing time to think, a side benefit), but be patient because someone *will* jump in! The more common problem is that more than one person jumps in at the same time. Let students know ahead of time that you will wait for someone to jump in, that there may be some quiet thinking time, and that if two or more people jump in at the same time, the person sitting closest to the door (or window or chalkboard) will read.

Popcorn reading. Students take turns reading aloud. One person begins, then, like popcorn popping in a pan, they toss the reading task to another student by saying, "Pop to [student's name]." Because of the fear factor—fear of being called on when not feeling confident, fear of being the last to be chosen or not chosen at all—this isn't much of an improvement over round-robin reading. However, you can overcome this problem by announcing the day before that you will be using this technique and that they will be able to sign up on the chalkboard to be tomorrow's "popcorn readers." Students can rehearse ahead of time if they choose, thereby giving them added exposure to the content. If they don't wish to read aloud at all, they have the option of not signing up.

Punctuation pause. This technique elicits laughter and lightheartedness because students take turns reading *only* to the next punctuation mark. The most that any student has to read is one sentence. Most often, it is only a phrase, sometimes just a word. Even the weakest of readers find this technique accessible.

Paired reading. Ahead of time, choose pairs of students who work well together. In addition to the usual social and behavioral concerns, take care to pair weaker readers with stronger readers. Members of each pair establish a plan for reading the passage—who will read what, whether they will read in unison, how the turn-taking will progress. Assure students that it is expected that they help each other out with words and ask each other questions about what they do not understand.

Radio call-in show. This is a bit of a gimmick and takes a few props, but it generates a lot of excitement about reading and thinking. Ask one student to prepare to be the host. His job is to read the text aloud to the class, pausing to take "calls" from listeners. Seat the host at a table in the front of the room and equip him with a set of earphones and a microphone (nonworking) so he looks the part. Give three or four students phones—old cell phones, old-fashioned dial phones, whatever you find in your basement or at a yard sale. They will "call in" with questions about what the host has just read. Everyone follows along as the host reads. It might go something like this:

> HOST: This is [*student's name*] at WHMS and I'm hosting today's show about the Lewis and Clark Expedition. Follow along as I read to you from page 52. [*Host reads a passage.*] Hold on. I see our switchboard is lighting up. Caller 1, what's your question?
>
> CALLER 1: I'm confused. What year did you say the Expedition started?
>
> HOST: [*Responds with the answer.*] An important question. Caller 2, what's your question?
>
> [*And so forth.*]

After the callers have phoned in their questions, they pass the phones to other students, who become the callers in the next segment of the read-aloud. As the questioning continues, callers might pose questions that the host cannot easily answer, questions about concepts that class members genuinely don't understand. If that happens, the host can call on his "special guest expert" (you) to clarify any misunderstanding. You'll slide into a chair next to the host and speak into the microphone, keeping the play alive.

RRAQ. Divide students into heterogeneous groups of four. Assign roles as follows:

> Student 1 *reads* a passage aloud to her group.
>
> Student 2 *retells* what he remembers.
>
> Student 3 *adds* other information that she remembers.
>
> Student 4 asks a *question* about what was read.

Assign the first role to a stronger reader. Role 4 is a comfortable position in which to place weaker readers. They will have the benefit of having heard the text read, hearing two people restate what was in the passage, and being expected to ask about something that might be difficult to understand. Everyone is involved; no one is at a disadvantage.

Variation and Choice

Pepper your classroom reading with a variety of techniques. Once you have introduced a number of them, allow students (within reason) to choose the ones they like. They may like one technique more than the others and may even invent techniques of their own. Be open to their suggestions. Offer them choices for their own reading as well. Some may choose to read silently, alone. Others may prefer to read alone but with a partner close by to offer help or discuss things. Others may want the security of having you at their side, ready to help. Variation brings liveliness to the classroom; choice allows students to own the processes.

We have used these techniques with hundreds of students and sought their opinions. They appreciate the variety and choice, and love it when the learning is active. The most gratifying feedback has come from the weaker readers. They consistently tell us that that these techniques make it okay to read more slowly and help them know what is important and how to think. These are reasons enough to continue to use them.

Here Today, Gone Tomorrow? Strategies That Help Students Retain Vocabulary

Write the word three [five, ten] times.

Look it up in the dictionary.

Write the definition.

Identify the part of speech.

Use it in a sentence.

Sound familiar? For the past fifteen years, we've asked teachers and teachers-to-be to recall how they were taught vocabulary. Even though they come from different regions of the country and are from different generations, they always recall this rote exercise. We remember the same procedure. They also sheepishly confess their ways of getting around this boring exercise:

- We wrote the first letter of the word three [five, ten] times down the page, then the second letter, then the third.

- We wrote the first definition—or the shortest.

- We wrote sentences like "I saw a _____" if it was a noun or "I will _____ tomorrow" if it was a verb.

- We just learned it for the test, then forgot it.

We remember doing the same things.

Why has this rote and robotic way of "doing" vocabulary persisted despite its inefficacy? It stems from good intentions—from teachers' innate understanding that vocabulary is critical. *Something* needs to be done about teaching vocabulary, and that something has most often been to fall back on the way we were taught—look it up, write the definition. . . . The steps *appear* to convey the meaning and provide common terminology for discussing content, but our own experience tells us this isn't so. Nevertheless, there are ways to make vocabulary acquisition exciting, effective, and accessible to all students.

■ All Vocabulary Is Not Created Equal

Although teachers' editions and curriculum guides provide lists of vocabulary, not all of that vocabulary deserves equal attention. Furthermore, not every word that your class needs will be on those lists, which are best guesses on the publisher's part. Only you can make the final decision. The first step is to look at your text and your class. Think about which words in the text deserve special attention, are important for these particular students. Next, decide what level of difficulty each of those words presents, because the tasks necessary for teaching each level are different.

We think of vocabulary in three levels, similar to Beck, McKeown, and Kucan's (2002) categorization of vocabulary into tier one, tier two, and tier three:

- *Level one* words are those found in students' listening and speaking vocabularies. They have heard and said them. For the most part, they require no preteaching, save for possibly noting any irregularities in spelling or pronunciation. An example would be *pneumonia*. They've heard of it, known people who have had it, and have even been threatened with it ("Zip up that coat or you'll catch pneumonia!"). Other than the caution, "By the way, *pneumonia* starts with a silent *p*. Don't pronounce it puh-neumonia!" no further teaching is likely to be necessary. Students should be able to understand level one words in context as they read.

- *Level two* words pose more of a challenge. They are not part of students' listening or speaking vocabularies. They have not heard or said these words before, but they are aware of a concept they can attach to them. Take *indigent*, for example. Students may not be familiar with this word, but they are familiar with a related concept: poor, needy, homeless. The task with level two words is to develop meaning relationships to familiar concepts.

- *Level three* words are the most complicated. Not only are they not in students' listening and speaking vocabularies, students probably don't know any related concepts. You must demonstrate, model, act these words out—do whatever it takes to develop both the concept and the vocabulary that names it. Specialized words (e.g., *ohm, Pangaea*) fall into the level three category.

■ Vocabulary Before and During Reading

The before stage of reading is critical. Fortunately, good before reading strategies—attending to prior knowledge, hypothesizing and predicting, and so on—can be matched with vocabulary instruction. As we find ways to help students hook new words to their prior knowledge, to hypothesize and predict about them, and as we equip them with the strategies they need to do so, we jump-start comprehension. Rather than being an isolated exercise, learning vocabulary becomes an integral part of making meaning.

In the activities that follow, vocabulary is *implanted* orally in conversation before students have to meet the words in text. This is important for all learners, but especially for those who are dealing with English as a second language or are having difficulty with reading.

Alphabet Splash

An "alphabet splash" is a quick way to get students to use their prior knowledge and hear and see words ahead of time. After you have identified the vocabulary you want to introduce, list the first letter of each word on a transparency. Have students brainstorm the words they think might be found in a chapter about the subject.

Let's say you're getting ready to read about maps and you've identified d*egrees,* e*quator,* l*atitude,* l*ongitude,* p*arallel,* and p*rime meridian* as key vocabulary. Write *D, E, L,* and *P* at the top of the page, and invite students to suggest words starting with these letters that they might find in a piece about maps. Accept all responses and write them under the appropriate letter. For *L,* students might say *lines, locations, length, little,* and *Lusitania.* Although not exactly what you are looking for, the words are their prior knowledge, their starting place. They're finding a "hook" for the new information. Even a response that seems far afield, like *Lusitania,* should be accepted and written down, because who knows what connection it may trigger later on. Of course, you want the words *latitude* and *longitude* to emerge, and they very well may. If they don't, however, you can say "I want to play, too!" and add these words, thereby implanting them.

Accepting students where they are in an activity like this is essential. You are asking them to engage in the critical reading skills of hypothesizing and predicting. In other words, they have to take a risk. A response from you like, "No, that's wrong, not going to be in there—a ridiculous guess" sends a message; the student is likely to think, *I'm not going to try again.* Students' prior knowledge is their prior knowledge. Their predictions are their predictions. We will change them through the reading, not through chastising them about their inability to guess better. We must not shut them down before they've even started.

Grouping to Predict

Here you offer students a group of familiar words from the text that they must connect to unfamiliar words from the same text through meaningful best guesses. First display a list that includes one or two level two (or level three) words, the rest being level one words. Then have students, in small groups, create meaningful groupings of these words. Here are the ground rules:

- The words in each group must relate to each other in some meaningful way.

- Each group must have at least three words.

- All words must be used.

- Words can appear in more than one group.

- Best guesses are encouraged when you don't know for sure!

In Karen Hesse's awarding-winning novel *Out of the Dust* (1997) about life in the Dust Bowl era, one of the central themes is the father's intractable refusal to accept crop diversification. He stubbornly waits for the wheat crop to yield. Only after untold tragedy does he finally consider planting other crops. *Diversification* might be a level two word, as might *sorghum*, the name of a crop. (However, if you are reading this with students who live in a farming area, these words would probably be level one—still more support for our contention that teachers who know their students must determine which words to teach!) A list of level one words might include *rain, dust, blowing, farmer, wind, shack, crops, ripped, dried, cotton, wheat, grit, grass,* and *hunger.* Now have students create word groupings from these level one and level two words. Because every word must be used in a group with at least two others, they will have to take their best guesses. After calling on their collective prior knowledge and taking a risk to hypothesize and predict, they will be ripe for meeting and understanding these words as they occur in the text.

Pull Out the Prop Box

Some words have to be defined ahead of time: try as you may, you can't think of any related concepts to use as a hook. These level three words require more effort to bring to life. A definition, a few props, and a bit of dramatics can do wonders. Take *Pangaea,* for example. Defined as the hypothetical supercontinent that existed 200 to 300 million years ago when all continents were joined, it likely is a word students will find hard to grasp conceptually. Develop the concept by giving each of seven students a card on which you have written the name of a continent. Then dip into your prop box and give each of them a little item to make their continent memorable. The person representing North America might receive an American flag; South America, a coffee cup; Europe, a miniature Eiffel Tower; Africa, a long strip of blue crepe paper (for the long, blue Nile); Asia, a teacup; Australia, a stuffed kangaroo; and Antarctica, a winter scarf. Have them stand, bunched together, in the front of the room. Ask the rest of the class to begin stamping their feet to indicate seismic activity, and to move their hands across their desks, skiing style, to indicate the shifting tectonic plates. As the rumbling continues, have the continents shift away from each other (except for Europe and Asia who continue to link arms) and move to their familiar Mercator-projection positions. Pangaea. Done.

About a Word

This is another good strategy to use when you feel you need to define a key word at the outset. Rather than leaving it at the definition, expand on it by building relationships. The format is simple. Have students divide a notebook page into four boxes labeled *definition, synonyms or highly related words, examples,* and *looks like,* while you do the same on a transparency, chart, or SMART Board (see Figure 3.1).

Here's an example of how it works using the word *renegade.* Its definition is *a person who deserts one cause for another.* After you provide the definition, lead students in brainstorming synonyms or highly related words: *traitor, deserter,*

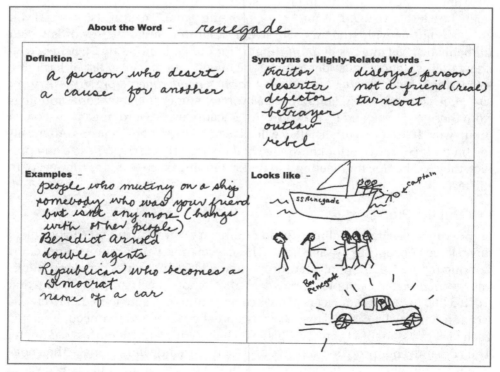

Figure 3.1. About the Word

defector, betrayer, outlaw, rebel, disloyal person, not a real friend, turncoat. Accept their slang terms, as long as they are school-appropriate, because these may be just the hooks they need to make the word their own. Then brainstorm examples: *people who mutiny on a ship, Benedict Arnold, double agents, somebody who used to be your friend but now is friends with other people, a Republican who becomes a Democrat.* A student might suggest the car model Renegade, which brings up some interesting questions. What image is the car maker trying to project? What kind of person might want to own such a car? Why? In the fourth box, *looks like,* students can sketch their own versions of a renegade, adding still another channel for learning.

Anticipations

This is a good strategy to use with text that is divided into sections with headings. Donna came up with it after she asked a group of students who were having difficulty reading their psychology textbook what they felt the problem was. They practically screamed, "The *terms*—too many, too fast." So she developed a list of terms they would encounter in the next reading assignment. She also divided a sheet of paper into boxes, one box for each section heading (see Figure 3.2). Then she had the students, in small groups, place each term in a box based on their best guesses.

Putting their heads together, the students placed obvious terms into the appropriate boxes (e.g., *hue* into *color, eye movements* into *visual receptors*) and speculated about differences between time and space interactions and terms that seemed to be tied to several headings. Prior knowledge about how words work (the prefixes *tri-* and *after-*) surfaced, and they discussed common associations they had with terms such as *image* and *saturation.* Ultimately, they simply guessed where to put some of the terms. Donna reassured them it was fine if their preliminary placements turned out to be incorrect, and she told them they would be able to return to their list later and make adjustments.

Afterward there was lots of talk about the terms, high fives for those they had guessed correctly, and smiling groans for those they hadn't. Students surprised themselves with how the vocabulary had come alive and how much stake they had in it!

Bank Deposits

Students use their best guesses in this activity as well (the financial wordplay gives a sense of fun to what could become a tedious look-up-vocabulary activity). Students draw on their prior knowledge and hypothesize about the "bank's assets," "depositing" them into matching "funds" before they read. After they read and confirm the definitions through the glossary, they deposit the words into the correct matching funds. Figure 3.3 is an example from Roberta's science class.

ANTICIPATIONS ...

You will encounter these words in the text:

✓ rods	✓ stabilized image	✓ negative afterimage
✓ saturation	✓ receptive fields	✓ brightness contrast
✓ phenomenon	✓ acuity	✓ duplexity theory - 2 places ?
✓ edges	✓ Mach bands	✓ lateral inhibition
✓ hue	✓ trichromatic color ?	✓ eye movements

BEFORE you read, take your best guess and place them in the boxes below. Under which of the following headings will these words occur?

The Visual Receptors

acuity
involuntary eye
           movements
receptive fields
rods
lateral inhibition

Interaction in Time: Adaptation

negative after image
duplexity theory ?
stabilized image
saturation

Interaction in Space: Contrast

phenomenon
edges
Mach bands
duplexity theory ?

Color

trichromatic
hue
brightness contrast

Figure 3.2. Anticipations

Science 7   Scientist _____ p. # _____

VOCABULARY—Natural Selection

DIRECTIONS:

1. BEFORE you look up the definitions, take a guess and deposit the words in the word bank into the column at the <u>left</u> with the best matching definition.

2. AFTER you use your glossary and textbook (pages 101–121) to define these words, put the correct words from the bank into the matching column on the <u>right</u>.

species	speculation	genetic variation
overproduction	Charles Darwin	generation time
mutation	selective breeding	adaptation
fossils	fossil record	evaluation
vestigial structures	trait	natural selection

BEFORE	DEFINITION	AFTER
	1. a characteristic that helps an organism survive in its environment	
	2. characterized by a group of organisms that can mate with one another to produce fertile offspring	
	3. the process by which populations accumulate inherited changes over time	
	4. the solidified remains or imprints of a once-living organism	

Figure 3.3. Bank Deposits (*continues*)

BEFORE	DEFINITION	AFTER
	5. a historical sequence of life indicated by fossils found in layers of the Earth's crust	
	6. the remnant of a once-useful anatomical structure	
	7. scientist who developed his theory of evolution by natural selection by observing nature	
	8. a distinguishing quality that can be passed from one generation to another	
	9. the breeding of organisms that have a certain desired trait	
	10. the process by which organisms with favorable traits survive and reproduce at a higher rate than organisms without the favorable trait	
	11. each species produces more off-spring than will survive	
	12. in a population of organisms, each individual has a unique combination of traits that sometimes increases its chances for survival and reproduction	
	13. a change in the order of the bases in an organism's DNA (changes in a gene)	
	14. the period between the birth of one generation and the birth of the next generation	
	15. the process by which two populations of the same species become so differ-ent that they can no longer interbreed	

Figure 3.3. *Continued*

Moveable Categories

Social studies teacher Marie writes her vocabulary words on cards with magnets attached to the back and places them on the whiteboard at the beginning of a unit. She invites students to move the words around and suggest categories into which the words might fit. Initially, students make rough cuts, such as "words we know" and "words we don't know" based on their prior knowledge (and lack thereof). With more discussion and encouragement of best guesses about other configurations, though, they begin to play with possibilities. "Maybe these two words are about communism." "Maybe these are places." Knowledge of affixes and word origins comes into play as they speculate about related words. As students encounter the vocabulary in context through reading and lecture, they continue to modify the groupings and categories to reflect their learning-in-progress.

Moveable Definitions

Here you combine the previous two activities into an interactive exercise. Make a set of magnetic vocabulary cards for your unit and another set of magnetic cards containing the definitions. Laminate both sets so you can reuse them from year to year. At the opening of the unit, have students speculate about word meanings by arranging the word cards on the whiteboard based on their best guesses. As the unit progresses and knowledge builds, match the definition cards with the appropriate words.

"Cut-able" Categories

It's no accident that our ten-digit phone numbers are grouped into three, three, and four digits. Remembering ten unrelated numbers would be difficult. The rhythmic grouping of area code (234), exchange (345), and personal number (2468) finds an easier home in our memories. Share this memory technique with your students by inviting them to find meaningful three- or four-word vocabulary groupings. Roberta adapted this cooperative learning activity from colleague Sarah, tweaking it to make it her own, just as you will (see Figure 3.4).

Students create six columns by folding a separate piece of paper into thirds (three columns on the front, three on the back) and using it to display their work. Roberta tells them to cut the words apart and arrange them in meaningful groups of three or four. She encourages students to play with the words, discuss them, and move them around until students have established groups that make sense to them based on their prior knowledge. (The only parameter she sets is that they cannot put the words in alphabetical order; she wants students to be focusing on meaning.) Students also determine an order for the words in each group and then glue these groups of words in column 1.

In column 2, students write their justifications for creating the groups. Many students list scientific categories (states of matter, changes of state). As one young man glued his words in column 1, he told Roberta he was grouping them into "hot

Chemist _____ p. # _____

Vocab—Chapter 2

Brain research shows that grouping words in a way that makes sense to you makes them easier to learn! Let's make learning easier!

YOUR JOB: You will work in <u>cooperative</u> groups of 2 to 4 students. Be sure to complete each task before moving onto the next!

1. Cut out the words found in the box at the bottom of this page. Be neat! You and your group need to arrange and rearrange these words into groupings that make sense to you. Next, glue these words in your groupings and order in the first column of the next page.

2. Once this is finished, use column 2 to write the reason for the order and grouping of words.

3. Use your glossary to write the definition of each word in column 3. Reminder—be neat!

4. In column 4, draw an illustration for that word.

5. In column 5, write a paragraph using at least ten of these vocabulary words. The paragraph can be factual (nonfiction) or embedded in a piece of fiction that is silly or humorous. However, be sure to use all words appropriately! (This paragraph must be at least five sentences long.) <u>Underline</u> each of the vocab words in your paragraph.

6. Finally, make a prediction in column 6. Write at least three sentences predicting what our lab may be like.

solid	sublimation	boiling
plasma	freezing	liquid
condensation	evaporation	melting
change of state	gas	vaporization
states of matter		

Figure 3.4. "Cut-able" Categories

words," "cold words," and "shun words." She was puzzled by the "shun" words until he explained that they were words he didn't know for sure, but they all ended with -*tion*. Students' prior knowledge is their prior knowledge, so she let it go!

Columns 3 and 4 require students to look up the words in the glossary to confirm meaning, write their definitions, and illustrate them. Because they have made a best-guess commitment to the vocabulary, they respond with assorted "ahas," "oops," and "got its" as they work through these phases.

Column 5 brings forth a flurry of creativity. Roberta is always pleasantly surprised by the results. Generally, about half the students, instead of writing factual science essays, write stories that include the vocabulary in lifelike settings— someone buying a Popsicle in a market on a hot day, friends playing on the beach, scientists talking about an experiment they are conducting. The inclusion of characters, thoughts, and feelings brings the vocabulary to life. By the time students reach column 6, they are ready to predict with reasonable accuracy what the lab session they are about to participate in will be about.

Playful Stories

Stories have great power in helping students apply a meaningful layer of understanding to new words.

Break it down. Breaking down is perfectly all right in school, as long as you're breaking down words, not having a psychological meltdown! Having difficulty understanding natural selection? Think about the noun form of *natural*: *nature*. Think about the verb form of *selection*: *select*. Put the two words together and you have "nature selects." What is a carnivore? Invite your Spanish speakers to explain that *carne* means *meat*, so a *carnivore* is a meat eater.

Tell a silly story. Making up stories, as long as they are not mean-spirited, to help remember what words mean is also effective. Can't remember the difference between *mitosis* (cell reproduction in body cells) and *miosis* (cell reproduction to produce egg and sperm cells)? Invent a story! Mitosis happens in "my toesies" and my toes are part of my body. When Roberta's class was confusing the symbols for silver (Ag) and gold (Au), a student solved the problem by saying, "Ag stands for silver because it *a*in't gold!" No one confused them again.

Tell it to spell it. Stories help cement correct spelling as well. When students lament, "I just can't spell this word!" chances are that they *can* spell a good bit of it correctly but fall apart in a certain section. Introduce them to BME analysis— beginning, middle, end. Where is the error? In the beginning, middle, or end?

Once the trouble spot is identified, help them create a "breakdown" story about it. For example, if the middle of the word *revolution* trips them up because of the schwa sound in the second syllable (is it *rev-a-lution*, *rev-e-lution*, or *rev-o-lution*?), have students think about what people are doing in the revolution— *revolting*. They hear the *o* sound in *revolting* and retain it in the inflected form of the word. Similarly, concentrating on *incline* can inform the spelling of *inclination*, remembering *muscular* will help them spell *muscle*, and so on.

When breaking down a word and reflecting on a related one doesn't work, silly stories can provide a useful mnemonic clue. What about that ending syllable in the word *relevant*. Is it *-ant* or *-ent*? A story about how buying a *van* was a *relevant* decision for a large family can help. Many of us grew up on stories about the *principal* being our *pal*, and how there is *a rat* in the middle of *separate*, both time-honored examples of this kind of mnemonic. The best silly stories, we have found, are those created by the students themselves, after they've identified the location of their error.

■ Vocabulary After Reading

After reading, students need to solidify their knowledge of vocabulary. While best guesses and predictions are appropriate *before* reading, we expect students to know the vocabulary and concepts *afterward*. The following activities can help.

The 4Cs: Checking, Confirming, Changing, Clarifying

An obvious activity is to return to the best guesses made during the before stage. Revisit, and celebrate, the connections that students made early on, then discuss how mature readers modify these best guesses after reading. It is so easy to lapse into "Hey! We got that one right!" and "Boy, we really blew it on that one." Avoid these judgments. Instead, couch comments in terms of the 4Cs of good readers:

- They *check* on their understandings.

- They *confirm* where they were on the right track.

- They *change* their earlier predictions that have been informed through the reading.

- They *clarify* anything about which they are still unsure.

The 4Cs reinforce the overall reading process, making it okay to have initially guessed incorrectly. It's a normal part of learning. Judgment calls of "right" and "wrong" suggest that it's really just been a game of rewarding the strong and punishing the weak all along.

Possible Paragraphs

List on the board three to six key vocabulary words from the unit. Give students a brief time in which to write a paragraph that uses all the words meaningfully. They should attempt to show relationships among the words, not just list definitions. Students can do this in pairs, then share their paragraphs to see how other students have incorporated the words.

Rap Writing

If your students are into rap, invite them to write their vocabulary words in that genre. They will enjoy performing their original raps for the class, and the repetition of the words as each rapper performs will help solidify everyone's understanding. Print out the raps and add still more exposure to the words by having students circle the words on the papers.

Vocabulary Circles

Encourage students to think about their vocabulary from the inside out. In the example in Figure 3.5, students are asked to think of descriptors that relate to a given term, then use their descriptors in writing a paragraph that defines the term.

You can specify the parts of speech to be used as descriptors (e.g., one noun, one verb, one adjective) or leave it open. You can divide the circles into as many or as few compartments as you like, depending on how many descriptors you want students to use.

Variations include:

- Give students who are having difficulty "starter" descriptors in each circle (one of the three, two of the four, all of them).

- Provide the written paragraph and have students extract the key terms to place in the circles.

Missing Pieces

Challenge students to think about vocabulary in terms of both definition and example by having them fill in the missing pieces. Prepare a three-column chart with the headings *vocabulary word*, *definition*, and *example*. Provide the vocabulary word, the definition, or an example, then have students fill in the rest. In Figure 3.6, students are given the words *continent* and *archipelago* and must define and provide an example for each. *Country* and *peninsula* are defined, but students must provide the term and an example. *Hemisphere* is neither named nor defined; students must discern the term and definition by looking at the example.

Pick a Card

Write each vocabulary word on a card. On the back of each card, write the definition of a different vocabulary word. (This sounds counterintuitive, but read on.) Call on students to pick a card from the deck until there are no cards left. Choose one student to come forward, display the vocabulary word on his card, and ask for the definition. The student holding the correct definition goes to the front of the room, reads it to the class, turns the card over to display the next word, and asks for the definition. This continues until all vocabulary words have been presented and their definitions shown.

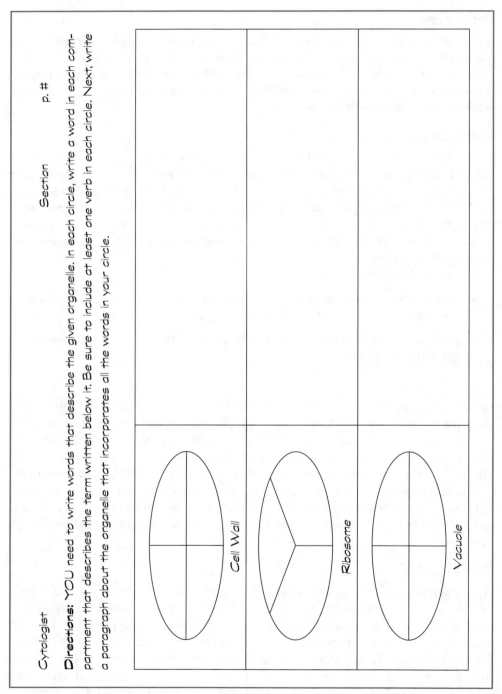

Figure 3.5. Vocabulary Circles

VOCABULARY WORD	DEFINITION	EXAMPLE
1. continent		
2.	A nation or an independent state	
3.		
4. archipelago		
5.	Body of land almost entirely surrounded by water but connected to the mainland by an isthmus	

Figure 3.6. Missing Pieces

Add some excitement by timing this activity. (Roberta uses a large stopwatch on her SMART Board, accessible through stopwatch.com, to make the elapsed time extremely visible.) Record the time for the first round, then have students pass their cards to others who didn't play in the first round. Play again and record the time. Challenge the students to improve their time each round. Students beg to play this game, and Roberta never wants for volunteers. It gets them up and moving, having fun, and reinforcing vocabulary all at the same time.

Predict Test Questions

Have students, in small groups, take a vocabulary list and construct a quiz based on the words. Then have them switch papers with another group, answer the questions, and return the papers to the original group to be scored. Ask members of each group to pick their best question and list it on a chart. Promise to use at least one of these questions on the next test. Depending on the nature of the tests you give or the kind of test-taking strategy you are teaching, you can specify that students create multiple choice, true/false, matching, fill-in-the-blank, or short-answer questions. Understanding how questions are structured by *writing* them will pay dividends in test-taking as well as understanding vocabulary.

■ Vocabulary Always: Word Walls Grow Up

We hope the vocabulary we teach will stay with our students forever, not just until the next quiz. But how do we keep it alive throughout the year? Perhaps we can take some cues from our primary grade colleagues, whose classrooms display word work all year long.

Commonly used in beginning reading to introduce and review basic sight vocabulary, word walls are a staple in early elementary school classrooms. As the name suggests, they are word cards affixed to a wall, generally in alphabetical order. Teachers lead students in assorted activities with these words to develop basic skills. Why should fun with vocabulary stop at the end of the early grades? Word walls can grow up right alongside the students.

Instead of arranging vocabulary words in alphabetical order, do so by unit or subject, with each set of words displayed on a different color of eighteen-inch by twenty-four-inch poster board. Type or print each word on white paper (for contrast). Hang them up high so everyone can see them and you can play with them all year. Then, get ready for fun.

Guess What's Inside My Head

This activity is a lot of fun and takes just a couple of minutes. Students have five clues in which to guess what's inside your head. They number their papers 1 through 5. The first clue is always, "It's on the [color] word wall." The second, third, and fourth clues pertain to analysis of the word (phonics, roots, syllables, compounds, prefixes/suffixes, even the part of speech). The fifth clue is always, "It fits into this sentence: _____."

Here's an example using the word *Pangaea*:

Guess what's inside my head!

Clue 1: It's on the red word wall.

Clue 2: It has three syllables.

Clue 3: It contains a soft /g/ sound.

Clue 4: Its first syllable means *all* in the Greek language.

Clue 5: It fits in this sentence: *A supercontinent from the late Paleozoic Era is known as* _____.

Guess What's Inside My Head is a way to reinforce vocabulary and practice word analysis. You can play with words from previous units to review past vocabulary, play the game with the present unit to reinforce current vocabulary, or use words from future units to "implant" vocabulary that's to come.

A Technological Twist

Roberta adds technology to the word walls concept by projecting PowerPoint slides that have different-color backgrounds depending on the unit or topic. Students label six lines on their paper, 1 through 6, and respond to these instructions:

1. Choose a background color.

2. Choose a word from the list.

3. Choose a word with [number] syllables.

4. Choose a word that means _____.

5. Write the word and its definition.

6. Use the word in a sentence.

The extra steps of writing and defining the word in their own terms and using it in a sentence are time-honored requests.

Sometimes Roberta adds another challenge as instruction 7: think of other words related to the identified term. The conversations that ensue are always interesting. The word *electron*, for example, led to a rich semantic network that included *electric, electronic, electrode, electricity,* and *electrician*. Then a student asked, "What about *election*?" This query sent the class to the Internet to look up the origins of both *electron* (which comes from the Greek for *amber*) and *election* (which comes from the Latin for *equivalent to*).

The Alphabet Chart Grows Up

Go into a first-grade classroom and you'll find alphabet cards parading across the wall over the chalkboard. At that grade level, the cards usually show the correct handwriting formation and include a picture of something that starts with that letter. Handwriting formation and phonics understandings are a big part of early learning. When those skills are mastered, the alphabet cards tend to disappear. Perhaps we should resurrect them and repurpose them for the upper grades.

Instead of focusing on formation and phonics, the alphabet cards could display content vocabulary. At the end of each unit, add the new words beneath the appropriate letter. When you have a minute here and there, play with past words: *Tell me an* R *word that we learned in our Civil War study . . . a* C, D, *and* T *word from* Number the Stars *. . . a word you can't quite remember . . . a noun and a verb from our safety unit.* This takes very little time and keeps cumulative vocabulary from slipping away.

■ Active, Fun Vocabulary

Vocabulary is important, and the process of learning new words can be active and fun if we approach it right. If the urge to tell students to *write it down, look it up, write the definition, identify the part of speech, and use it in a sentence* strikes you again, resist! Instead, try a strategy from this chapter, or invent your own. Keep it active, and make it playful!

CHAPTER

Inviting Writing: Helping Students Understand Content

Do you resist including more writing in your classes because all you can think of are more papers to grade, more complaints to hear when you assign them, and more headaches to buffer when you get home? If so, chances are you might be equating writing—essays, reports, term papers—with the end product only, the kind of writing that goes through many stages to produce a polished final piece.

That is not what this chapter is about. What we advocate here is the kind of writing that adds up to a lot of learning—a way of thinking, a way of figuring out what you think and what you know. This writing is brief, but there is lots of it, and most of it ungraded (did your ears perk up?). This kind of writing is the most natural thing in the world to include in your classes, and when you do, your students' understanding will soar.

Roberta's classes do a lot of short, quick writing. Her students write almost every day: they think aloud on paper, monitor their understanding, and discover what they know. They write to review, to sum up, and to ask for help. Writing provides time for the mind to process information and is a pathway to *thinking*, just as talking, reading, and self-reflection are. It is a natural fit with content, particularly for those who need extra time to learn.

This kind of writing invites everyone in. Each student writes for an audience of him- or herself, a trusted audience that will understand even the briefest attempts at describing concepts, even if they are misspelled, in another language, or grammatically incorrect. It is writing to *learn*, not to produce a finished product. In the process, students do a lot of thinking. Sometimes this thinking is collaborative—students talking together as they wrestle with meaning before they write. But in the end, each student must do her or his own writing, in her or his own voice, for herein lies the power of personally coming to know. Periodically, this kind of writing may be shared with peers or the teacher, but it is generally not evaluated.

Students' overall literacy improves as well. When students write for a safe audience of self, peers, or a trusted adult, they practice moving the hand across the page, find their voice, and become a more fluent writer. As they create text from the inside out, they deepen their understanding of how texts work. When they read back what they have written, they get additional exposure not only to the content being taught but also to the processes of reading. The English/language arts teachers will thank you profusely for helping hone these processes in your classes. Your students should, too, because you are developing an aptitude they will carry with them the rest of their lives.

■ Jotting for Understanding

Some call them journals or writer's notebooks; others call them learning logs. Regardless of the name, they are notebooks in which students write their thoughts and experiment with craft without fear of being graded. We call them *jottings*, and students make them in the same notebooks in which they have taken notes on the subject matter. The name *jottings* connotes the kind of writing we envision—short, snappy, capture-that-thought-before-it-leaves-you. It goes beyond the one- or two-word "bellringers" (write your answer quickly before the bell rings) often found on classroom whiteboards. It is writing that expresses complete thoughts and integrates use of vocabulary in a meaningful way. Jottings may also include visual representations (graphs and the like) that express something students have learned.

Hidden Treasures in Your Teacher's Edition

Most teacher's editions that accompany student texts contain possible writing assignments for each unit of study. They often appear as options for end-product, graded writing. With a bit of repurposing, they can become worthy fodder for jottings. Roberta selects and modifies a useful one and projects it on a screen as the class enters the room. The students read the prompt and respond while she takes care of attendance and other administrivia necessary to start each period.

Here are some examples she has adapted from the Holt Science and Technology Series (2002) (she provides a scaffold by underlining the key task):

- Which of the following best describes a living cell?

    a. a building block

    b. a living organism

c. a complex factory

d. all of the above

<u>Write a paragraph</u> in your jottings defending your choice.

[Students select a multiple-choice answer but also justify it in writing.]

- Most cactuses have spines, which are leaves modified to protect the plant. The spines cover a juicy stem that stores water. <u>Explain</u> how cactus leaves and stems might have changed through the process of natural selection.

  [Presented the day after a lesson on natural selection, this prompt asks students to review their notes and apply what they have learned.]

Notebooks aren't just for words; students can also create various graphic features like those found in their textbook. (Most content-area texts include diagrams, charts, time lines, and the like.) Having students create these graphic features themselves develops their ability to read features created by others. After exploring diagrams depicting natural selection, Roberta greeted the class with this challenge, one they could complete as homework over two days:

Squirrels — The Survivors

<u>Create a diagram (with pictures and words)</u> that outlines the process of change for a population of squirrels (black, red, gray, and white) marooned on a treeless island of black sand that is also home to squirrel-eating foxes.

Jottings are a good investment during the few minutes spent "settling in" at the beginning of class. Then, after students quickly share, either with a partner or the whole class, Roberta is able to clear up any misunderstandings, congratulate the writers, and segue into her next lesson. It is a good "before" activity, connecting yesterday with today. It's active learning; everyone is involved. It's brief, ungraded, and relatively painless. Take a good look at your teacher's edition. What treasures does it hold for you?

Quotations

Once she was committed to using jottings, Roberta found significant prompts in all sorts of places. She found this wordy quote by Charles Darwin on the Internet and thought it begged to be shortened:

Whenever I have found that I have blundered, or that my work has been imperfect, and when I have been contemptuously criticized, and even when I have been overpraised, so that I have felt mortified, it has been my greatest comfort to say hundreds of times to myself that "I have worked as hard and as well as I could and no man can do more than this." (Darwin and Regal 2005, 52)

Here was an opportunity to have students get to the essence of a message, figure out the main idea. She projects this quotation and asks, "What message was Darwin trying to give?" After clarifying confusing vocabulary, she sends students off to jot down their ideas and share them with a partner.

Then she challenges them to this task: *It took Darwin 68 words to deliver this message. You are to* write *the same message in* fifteen words or less! Students put their heads together, carefully consider every word in their original jottings, counting them out loud. From the class discussion that follows, it is clear they got Darwin's point. So Roberta invokes a bit of pop culture: "Nike says a similar thing in three words—Just. . . ." The class responds in unison, *"Do it!"* The spirit of Darwin's message has taken root.

A jotting in Roberta's classes on the scientific method was prompted by the words of noted immunologist Melvin Cohn (1994, 2): "I am fortunate to be in a profession where the realization of being wrong is equivalent to an increase in learning." What a strong statement about the work of scientists!

We all have major players in our field, people whose insights capture the essence of our content. Who are yours? A famous general? An athlete? A mathematician? An author reflecting on his writing process? The Surgeon General? From time to time you come across comments that provoke your thinking. Or perhaps people make observations that are off base or misinformed. All are food for thinking through jotting.

Comics, Political and Otherwise

We often spot cartoons or comic strips that speak to our subject, chuckle, then lay the newspaper aside. Instead of sending these gems to the recycling bin, we should cut them out and bring them into our classroom. The topical issues and plays on language underlying cartoons and comics can jump-start student writing and discussions. They are wonderful ways to help students see relationships between science, current events, politics, and language. Roberta uses comics to spark students' writing about the conditions necessary for fungi to grow, the charge of atomic particles, how gravity affects baseballs, and how oil and politics are related. She often posts jokes related to her topics, the cornier the better, on her SMART Board without revealing the punch line and asks students to provide one. Then she ceremoniously scrolls down slowly . . . slowly . . . to reveal the punch line so students can compare what they wrote with the original. The topics and the writing are academic, but the beginning of class is fun.

If you are teaching government and civics during an election year, each class could begin with an editorial cartoon capturing a hot topic or blooper. Not teaching current events? You can find political cartoons going back to the 1800s by doing a bit of research on the Internet or in a library.

Jottings by Another Name: Exit Slips

Roberta likes the idea of jottings because they stay in the students' notebooks, as important as the official notes they take during her lectures and demonstrations. It's *their* thinking about *her* thinking, and it's a powerful way for them to monitor their learning. Other teachers vary the jottings idea by using them as "exit slips"—separate pieces of paper on which students respond to prompts and hand them in before leaving class. The exit slips are a way to gather information on students' comprehension, readiness levels, interests, or learning processes. The slips bring closure to that day's learning and provide useful information that can help guide future lessons and make decisions about how to best meet individual and group needs.

Some of these prompts are very straightforward:

- We are studying alliteration.

  List two examples of alliteration we found in _____.

  1.

  2.

- Today we investigated density and flotation.

  1. List three things you learned.

     a.

     b.

     c.

  2. Write at least one question you still have about this topic.

- Math exit slip for today:

  Is a square a rectangle? Explain your answer.

  With a bit of imagination, though, it's easy to add a little flair:

- Count Down to the Great Depression

  <u>Three facts</u> I learned about the Great Depression:

  1.

  2.

  3.

Two causes of the Great Depression:

1.

2.

One way in which people tried to survive:

1.

- For *one minute only*—and I'm timing!—write everything you remember about [topic of that day's class].

- List the Top Ten (à la David Letterman)

This is particularly fun for partners or small groups and is based on an idea by Barry Lane (2003). We laughed a lot as we created the top ten reasons to be a political platform:

10. You get associated with a lot of famous politicians.

9. You get introduced at a big convention that is lots of fun.

8. You can be either a Republican or a Democrat.

7. You get to be on television, the radio, and the Internet.

6. You might even have a blog dedicated to you where people can write in and talk about you.

5. Some people say there is a lot of hot air around you, so you'll never be cold.

4. You stand for good things.

3. Even if the politicians don't follow through with you, it's not your fault. You meant well.

2. You're part of the United States political system.

And the number one reason to be a political platform is

1. You encourage people to get out and vote.

The variations are endless, limited only by your creativity: the top ten characteristics of, reasons for, uses of, types of, causes of, contributors to, rules for, arguments against. . . .

- Vamp on numbers and days of the week: The Fab Five, The Thrilling Three, Two for the Teacher, The Friday Four, The Thursday Three, The Wednesday Whats, Two for Tuesday, Minimal Monday [only one response needed].

- Manipulate math to determine how many facts students must include. Roberta sometimes asks a student to pick a number between one and ten.

Let's say he picks five. Then she asks another to do the same. Let's say she picks two. Roberta adds them together and tells them to write seven facts. Of course, they catch on quickly and the number two starts to appear often—until she starts squaring or cubing it to get the count!

- Manipulate sports numbers. *Your favorite player on* x *team is number 26? 2 + 6 = 8. Give me eight facts. Your team won 21 to 14 yesterday? Subtract, and give me seven ideas.* When the numbers get large, Roberta often has students evaluate their work and star their three most important facts and share these. This leads to revision, as they reconsider their work, adding and deleting.

Jottings and exit slips are very useful for getting students to reflect on their learning processes as well as content. Simple stems allow students to reflect on and monitor their thinking:

I still wonder . . .

I don't understand . . .

I had the feeling that . . .

This reminded me of . . .

If I had been there, I would have . . .

I was surprised . . .

Maybe . . .

What is . . .?

I liked . . .

This got me thinking that . . .

What if . . .?

I used to think . . . but now I know . . .

A reading strategy I used was . . .

To better understand this, I need . . .

A word of caution: If you are using this kind of writing as exit slips, be absolutely clear that you will not be grading them. Students hand them in only to help you be a better teacher. Write nothing on them. And by all means refer back to them in subsequent classes. "I saw from your exit slips that you have a good understanding of blank, that you're still unsure about blah-bah-dee-blah, that a lot of you are confused about thus-and-so." Without this context, the writing can easily become a pop quiz by another name. This isn't what we want.

Group Jot-Arounds

Middle school language arts teacher Linda Rief, author of *100 Quickwrites* (2003) and *Seeking Diversity: Language Arts with Adolescents* (1991), has a passion for inspiring and encouraging teen writers. She uses group *write-arounds* (Roberta calls them *jot-arounds*) to get her students to collaborate as they come to terms with their understandings and misunderstandings. A write-around is somewhat like the traveling tale commonly used in elementary classrooms, in which each student starts a story, writes until time is called, then passes the story to the next person, who reads the first part and adds to the action, and so on, student to student to student.

Rief has her students work in groups of four. Students date their notebooks and write for two or three minutes about a book they've all read—what they are thinking about, questioning, or wondering. At Rief's signal, they pass their notebooks to the right. Each person reads the entry(ies) written by the previous group member(s) and then adds his or her own thinking, questioning, and wondering. On the fourth pass, the notebooks return to the original owners, who read what everyone else has written and add any final thoughts. Rief then asks the class to tell what issues and topics were raised during the writing, lists them on the board, and asks students to reflect on what they learned about and from each other.

In a content area, the prompt for writing might be to list what you know, to reflect on process, or both. Time is limited, so no one is expected to write a tome. Both those who write well and those who don't are able to contribute. It's okay not to know it all and to ask about what is confusing.

Octofacts

In this variation of a group jot-around, Roberta challenges students, in groups of eight, to come up with eight facts that they think will be on the test—hence the name *octofacts*. Each student begins with a separate piece of paper, and then follows the directions that Roberta projects onto the SMART Board:

- Write one fact that you must remember for the test. (Use a complete sentence.)

- Pass your paper to the left.

- Read the paper you just received.

- Write another important item to remember for the test.

- Pay attention. You may not repeat a fact!

- Write neatly. Other people need to read this.

- Keep going until *each* paper has eight facts.

After each group has amassed their facts, Roberta projects her own list of facts that she wants them to review. Sometimes her list duplicates items that students have written; sometimes not. The duplications cement their importance, while the new facts introduce additional critical information.

■ Using Mentor Texts

In elementary classrooms, mentor texts scaffold student writers, who examine the stylistic aspects of published authors, authors they love, and students emulate the authors in their own writing. Lynne Dorfman and Rose Cappelli's books (2007, 2009) are filled with examples of how teachers can use these books to "help writers notice things about an author's work that is not like anything they might have done before, and empower them to try something new" (2007, 3). Studying mentor texts improves student writers' voices and help bring a sense of story into writing about content. Although these mentor texts most often are picture books, they needn't be dismissed as inappropriate in secondary grades. On the contrary, their brevity makes them ideal for quick jottings about their content. Once you realize the power of such texts, you will never look at a children's book in the same way!

The Important Book

Beloved children's author Margaret Wise Brown's *The Important Book* (1949) is a wonderful mentor text. Key characteristics of such everyday things as a spoon, a daisy, the rain, grass, snow, an apple, and the sky are presented in a style appropriate for young children. Here's an example:

> The important thing about the sky is that it is always there.
> It is true that it is blue,
> and high,
> and full of clouds,
> and made of air.
> But the important thing about the sky is that it is always there. (n.p.)

Young children delight in the repetition of the first and last lines, but what Brown is really doing is reinforcing superordinate and subordinate concepts. You can borrow the framework and apply it to your content area, first by asking students to list five important things about the topic under study and to star the most important. Then, using the simple scaffold in Wise's book, they can translate their thoughts into text.

Here's an example:

> List five important things about the branches of government. Star (*) the most important.

1. Executive branch—the President
2. Legislative branch—Congress
3. Judicial branch—the courts
4. Checks and balances
5. They should work together

Using the stem "the important thing about the branches of government is" and the starred item on your list, write a complete sentence stating what is most important.

> The important thing about the branches of the government is that there are checks and balances.

Now turn the items on your list into complete sentences:

> The executive branch includes the President of the United States.
>
> The legislative branch includes Congress, which makes the laws.
>
> The judicial branch includes the courts, which interpret the laws.
>
> All three branches should work together.
>
> But the important thing about the branches of government is that there are checks and balances.

If You're Not from the Prairie . . .

David Bouchard paints a lyrical word picture of prairie life in *If You're Not from the Prairie . . .* (1993):

> If you're not from the prairie,
> You don't know the sun,
> You *can't* know the sun.
> > Diamonds that bounce off crisp winter snow,
> > Warm waters in dugouts and lakes that we know,
> > The sun is our friend from when we are young,
> > A child of the prairie is part of the sun.
> If you're not from the prairie,
> You *don't* know the sun. (6)

Succeeding pages, using the repetitive structure "If you're not from the prairie, you don't know," describe the wind, sky, flatness, grass, snow, trees, cold, and one's soul as only prairie dwellers can know.

This scaffolding is a direct match for places and eras of study: *if you're not from the desert, Africa, the Middle Ages,* and so on. And with a slight twist, the format can work for people, real and fictional, as well. Here is an example Donna created about herself:

> If you don't know Donna Topping, you don't know shopping.
> You *can't* know shopping.
>> Word is, she moved to Lancaster County because of it.
>> The antiques! The outlets! The Central Market Shops! The malls!
>> A traveler, she contributes to the economy of any area she visits, and has been known to buy extra suitcases just to haul home her loot.
>> A coat, four purses, and a briefcase from Italy because it was *Italian* leather, for cryin' out loud!
>> She once flew home from Hungary—ten hours in the plane—holding fragile glassware on her lap. You just can't get that kind of stuff here.
>> The Visa people love her.
> If you don't know Donna Topping,
> You *don't* know shopping.

Who do you study in your classes? Or what? Think about the possibilities: *If you don't know latitude, alliteration, photosynthesis, the commutative property. . . .*

"How to Be" Poems

Writing "how to be" poems (Lane 2003) is fun and focuses attention on key attributes of a concept using a simple verb-object pattern. Here is one we composed:

How to Be a Raindrop

Be H_2O
Have twice as much hydrogen as oxygen
Need it to be not too cold, not too hot
Evaporate from lakes and oceans
Condense in clouds
Fall, fall
Drizzle or pound down
Call yourself precipitation
Moisten things
Help crops grow
Support lush life
Hydrate the body
Be part of the water cycle
Support the circle of life

Dredging the mind for the essence of a concept is more rewarding when the reason is to create something that's fun to read. Also, the brevity of the verb-object pattern invites everyone to participate. "How to be" poems fit any content area, any subject, any person, place, or thing.

Once upon a Time, The End

Barry Kloske's *Once upon a Time, The End (Asleep in 60 Seconds)* (2005) is a tale any parent can appreciate. In it, a tired father tells very abbreviated stories to a child who is determined to forestall his approaching bedtime by asking for more. Here is the much condensed Little Red Riding Hood, titled "Small Girl, Red Hood":

> Small girl
> Red hood
> Big wolf
> In the woods.
> Grandma's gone
> Wolf in her cap
> Girl at the door
> Tap, tap
> Big ears to hear
> Big eyes to see
> Big teeth to eat
> Girl better flee.
> Strong woodsman
> Just outside
> Spied a wolf
> Heard a girl's cries.
> Axe swung
> Wolf run
> And the battle won
> The woodsman said,
> "Wow, I'm really tired, how about you?" (8)

You don't have to be a parent to see the pattern. Undoubtedly, your students remember their own ways of stalling at bedtime. Kloske distills each tale down to its essential events, no frills, no extra words. This is something we hope our students can do after we've taught a lesson that involves any kind of sequence—plot structure, a procedure, a historical occurrence. After sharing one of Kloske's tales, challenge students to create a "tired parent" version. (And, no, it doesn't have to rhyme.)

An Island Grows

Using a repeating noun-verb pattern, Lola M. Schaefer tells of the birth of an island in *An Island Grows* (2006). Here is an excerpt:

> Magma glows.
> Volcano blows.
> Lava flows and flows and flows.
> An island grows. (n.p.)

From these few opening lines, you can see how the subject-verb pattern invites play. In one of our workshops, a group of teachers joined us in quickly creating the following piece about their current unit of study, the Civil War:

> Soldiers fight
> Blood spills
> Battles rage
> Union splits
> Slaves escape
> Confederacy shatters
> North wins
> South doesn't.

Naming Poems

In the Cree Indian tradition, people acquire their names by characteristics they exhibit or things they do. Donna, inspired by a Cree Indian naming poem called "Quiet Until the Thaw," from *The Wishing Bone Cycle* (Norman 1972), wrote the following naming poem about herself when she came home with a speeding ticket:

Speeder in Strasburg

Yes, her name tells about her.
In fact, she was going 57 mph in a 25 mph zone in Strasburg.
People know that she normally is a safe driver,
But sometimes she forgets to watch her speedometer.
It often happens when she's talking with a passenger,
   A friend who shares her life,
   Who likes to talk about the same things,
   Who laughs at all the right places,
   Who loves to have fun.
Or when the road is wide and straight,
   Too easy to speed on,
   Just like that street in Strasburg that day.
Then she saw the flashing lights and heard the siren.
The nice officer got out of his car and reminded her with a ticket.
One hundred-fifty-seven dollars later,
She vowed to pay more attention to her driving.
Let's hope.

Using a naming poem as a scaffold, students can review content by giving a name to it. Borrowing the words *yes, her [his, its] name tells about her [him, it], in fact*, and *people*, Donna and a group of teachers in a workshop quickly adapted the format to the study of Pennsylvania.

Pennsylvania—Home to Me

Yes, its name tells about it.
In fact, we call it "home."
People know that Pennsylvanians came from someplace else:
The Welsh
 The English
 The Dutch
 The Lenni-Lenape
Others call it home today, too:
 The Eagles
 The Steelers
 The Flyers
 The Sixers
 The Amish.
It has it all:
 Chocolate
 Pretzels
 Mushrooms
 Farming
 Burning hay.
The mountains, the rivers, the rolling hills, the stone barns.
My home!

A flurry of spontaneous talk flowed from this quickly written first draft. Do we really want the Amish grouped with the sports teams? Should we have a stanza on Pennsylvania's history? Did we get all the products? All the landforms? Should we include tourism? Without being told, the workshop participants moved naturally into revising the writing, reviewing what they knew, and categorizing that knowledge appropriately. Aren't these all things we want students to do?

We have used these mentor texts with elementary and secondary students and with adults. In every setting, they generate enthusiastic willingness to write and, more important, enthusiastic willingness to think through content learned. These jottings can stand alone—writing just for oneself to think aloud on paper, either individually, in pairs, or in groups. However, you'll find that your students want to share them, to read one another's, to post them in the room, or to create a class book. Don't hesitate to help them revise and edit them and put them on display! Subsequent readings and rereadings of the displayed products provide still more exposure to your content.

■ Using Poetry to Write with Precision

Poetry is a perfect way to get students to write about content with precision. Every word counts. Every word packs a punch. Every word must be carefully considered. Prose allows you to ramble, digress, elaborate. Not so, poetry. It is brief and to the point, so it forces students to focus only on the most important ideas. What a great way to get students to distill the essence of their understanding and create a summary. Like writing prompted by mentor texts, poetry is enjoyable and applicable to all content areas.

The previous paragraph contains ninety words. Here is the same information in a twenty-five-word acrostic based on the word *content*.

> **C**ontent understanding distilled,
> **O**nly key concepts stated.
> **N**o rambling possible.
> **T**erse and to the point,
> **E**very word counts.
> **N**o faking possible.
> **T**he ultimate summary.

When we use acrostics and other forms of poetry in our classes, we push students toward sophisticated thinking. We help them separate superordinate from subordinate concepts as they visit and revisit content, deciding what is most important to include because words are at a premium. The task ranks low on physical writing, but high on content and understanding. Conversation in pairs or small groups before writing can provide additional scaffolding, something that is useful for all students.

Sample Poetry Formats

Here are some sample poetry formats and examples from our own writing and that of our students:

Format: **Clerihews**
Line 1:   person's name
Line 2:   rhymes with line 1
Lines 3 and 4   rhyme with each other

Example: Benjamin Franklin
Heard lightning cracklin'
He got a kite and then a key
And invented electricity.

Format: **Preposition Poem**
Each line begins with a preposition.

Example: Here Comes the Butterfly!
Within my bed
On the branch
Until it's time
Like a baby chick
In an eggshell
With a lot of moving
Out of the chrysalis I come
Up in the air
Away I fly!

Format: **Contrast Poem**

Line 1 of each stanza: I used to be . . .
Line 2 of each stanza: But now I am . . .

Example: I used to be part of a cloud
But now I'm on the ground.
Everyone steps on my friends and me
Because we condensed and fell down.

Format: **"If I Were" Poem**

Poem starts and ends with "If I were . . ."

Example: If I were a latitude line,
I'd make sure to keep an equal distance from my brothers and
sisters.
I'd ring around the Earth and help people tell locations.
I'd look like one of the rungs on a ladder.
I'd report myself in degrees away from the equator.
I'd proudly state that I measured Philadelphia at forty degrees
north.
If I were a latitude line,
I'd be sad because I'm invisible and not a real line.

Format: **Five Senses Poem**

Five lines, one sense for each line.

Example: *Bullying*
Sounds like crying
Smells like sour milk
Tastes like brussels sprouts
Feels like bruises and cuts
Looks dumb
I'm not going to be a bully!

Format: **Definition Poem**

Each line starts with "[topic] is . . ."

Example: *Division*

Division is cutting up a pizza.

Division is lining up in pairs.

Division is getting into groups.

Division is making sure everybody gets the same number of cookies.

Division is getting into two teams.

Format: **Haiku**

A poem in seventeen syllables that usually deals with nature; expresses one thought or idea, and often has a surprise element in the last five syllables.

First line: five syllables

Second line: seven syllables

Last line: five syllables

Example: clouds in the distance

getting closer and darker

no school tomorrow

Format: **Poems for Two Voices**

A call-and-response poetic conversation, sometimes in the form of questions and answers; read aloud by two voices.

Example: *The Water Cycle*

[Voice #1]

Hey water! What are you doing?

            [Voice #2]

            I'm evaporating.

You're what?

            I'm turning into vapor.

But why?

            Because the sun is heating me up.

Where will you go?

            I will be movin' on up to the sky and one day become a cloud.

How will you become a cloud?

            I will condense.

Format: **Recipe Poems**

Facts reported in a recipe parody, an idea originated by Barry Lane (2003).

Example: Declarative Sentence Stew

Ingredients:

1 thought
1 subject
1 verb
1 object
1 capital letter
1 period
Commas (according to taste)
Other parts of speech (according to taste)

Directions:

1. Spread out a piece of paper to work on.
2. Using your thought, take the subject and place it on the paper.
3. Add the verb.
4. Next, add the object.
5. Sprinkle in adjectives, adverbs, pronouns, and prepositions according to taste.
6. Place the capital letter at the beginning of the sentence.
7. Place the period at the end.
8. Taste to see if you need a comma to break it up.
9. Place in your notebook and let it set overnight.
10. Check in the morning to see if it looks and tastes like you thought it would.

Format: **Diamante**

A diamond-shaped poem that moves from one concept to its opposite:

Line 1: one word (a noun, subject)
Line 2: two words (adjectives describing noun in line 1)
Line 3: three words (-*ing* or -*ed* words that relate to line 1)
Line 4: four words (first, two nouns that relate to line 1; then, two nouns that relate to line 7)
Line 5: three words (-*ing* or -*ed* words that relate to line 7)
Line 6: two words (adjectives describing line 7)
Line 7: one word (a noun, opposite of line 1)

Example:

slavery
horrible unfair
crying wanting picking
owners gin railroad hope
singing hiding praying
wonderful beautiful
freedom

Format: **Triolet**

An eight-line poem with a repeating pattern. Line 1 is repeated in lines 4 and 7; line 2 is repeated in line 8. Lines 1, 3, 4, 5, and 7 rhyme; lines 2, 6, and 8 rhyme.

Example: *Exceptions*

There are exceptions to Mendel's rules
Like multigene inheritance and incomplete dominance.
In one, all the genes are mixed in a pool.
There are exceptions to Mendel's rules.
The other, neither gene controls, they don't have the tools.
The things that break the rules have great prominence.
There are exceptions to Mendel's rules
Like multigene inheritance and incomplete dominance.

—Lauren (seventh grader)

Format: **Cinquain**

A five-line poem with the syllable pattern 2, 4, 6, 8, 2.

Example: *Adverbs*

Adverbs
modify verbs.
They tell how, when, where, why,
but they do not always end with
L-Y.

Format: **Rhyming Riddle**

A four-line riddle in which lines 2 and 4 rhyme.

Example: From birds in the sky
To fish in Lake Placid
I'm inside all cells
And my *A* stands for acid.
What am I? _____ (Answer: DNA)

—Aaron (seventh grader)

These formats have an inherent playfulness and they prompt a great deal of collaboration as students talk beforehand and compose together. As with mentor texts, these poems can stand alone as jottings or quickwrites, but they can easily be revised and edited for public sharing. The benefit of reading and rereading content is a real plus.

Roberta includes a poetry assignment in her genetics unit. Students select one, two, three, or four forms like those above and write poems that include information they have learned about genetics. (Roberta doesn't need to teach the forms; she only needs to mention them. Using districtwide email, she communicates with teachers in previous grades, even in other buildings, finds out what forms they taught, and goes from there. She also adapts the number of required poems to her students' ability levels.) Each poem is scored against a simple checklist:

Followed directions	2 points
Content about genetics	2 points
Scientifically accurate	*2 points*
Total for each poem	6 points

Because she is using this assignment to move beyond just jottings, Roberta also requires that students revise and edit their work. She awards the following points:

Neatness	3 points
Spelling	*3 points*
Total editing points	6 points

Her students love bringing poetic forms to bear on an academic subject. They willingly revise and edit, and look forward to seeing their work posted in her "Poetry Corner." Of course, they are just as eager to read their classmates' offerings, which adds still more exposure to genetics. It's a fabulous way to review content, and reading their classmates' poems offers multiple opportunities for students to hear and manipulate the unit vocabulary.

Found Poetry

Creating *found poetry* develops reading and writing skills while reinforcing content. Students take a piece of text and identify the key words or phrases. Lifting them out of the text, they arrange them into free verse, thus "finding" a poem within the piece of discursive prose. If using a text they can write in, they can underline these important words and phrases. Better yet, they can write them on a separate piece of paper, cut them apart, and then move them around into the most poetic arrangement. Along the way, you have many opportunities to sneak in some reading lessons. ("Now remember—italicized words are usually important ones. Words like *however* often signal a contrast between two important ideas. Watch for signal words like *first, most important, finally*.") And, of course, by creating a poem with your students, you overtly model both the reading and writing processes needed.

Consider how the following relatively dull informational piece from a linguistics text comes to life through found poetry:

The Role of the Larynx in Speech

The first point where the airflow from the lungs encounters a <u>controlled resistance</u> is at the <u>larynx</u>, a structure of muscle and cartilage located at the <u>upper end of the trachea</u> (or <u>windpipe</u>) (see figure 3.1). The resistance can be controlled by the <u>different positions and tensions in the vocal cords</u> (or <u>vocal folds</u>), two muscular bands of tissue that stretch from front to back within the larynx (see figure 3.2). During <u>quiet breathing</u> the <u>cords are relaxed and spread apart</u> to allow the free flow of air to and from the lungs. During <u>swallowing</u>, however, <u>the cords are drawn tightly</u> together to <u>keep foreign material from entering the lungs</u>. For <u>speech</u> the most important feature of the <u>vocal cords</u> is that they can be <u>made to vibrate</u> if the airflow between them is sufficiently rapid and if they have the proper tension and proximity to each other. This rapid vibration is called voicing (or phonation). The <u>frequency of vibration</u> determines the perceived pitch. Because the vocal cords of <u>adult males</u> are <u>larger</u> in size, their frequency of vibration is relatively <u>lower</u> than the frequency of vibration in females and children. The pitch of adult males' voices is thus perceived as lower than that of females and children. (Akmajian et al. 1990, 55)

The underlined words and phrases, when arranged as free verse, take on a lyrical air:

The Role of the Larynx in Speech

Controlled resistance
At the upper end of the trachea
(windpipe).
Different positions and tensions in the
vocal cords
(vocal folds).
Quiet breathing
Cords relax
Spread apart.
Swallowing
Cords drawn tight
Keep foreign material from the lungs.
Speech
Cords made to vibrate
Voicing
Phonation.
Frequency of vibration
Pitch
Adult males
Larger
Lower.

Think of it this way: There are two possible ways to give students an assignment that asks them to identify main ideas, find key supporting details, and write a summary.

Choice #1: Read the passage several times. Then underline the main ideas and key supporting details. Finally, write a summary. Proofread your work before handing it in for a grade.

Choice #2: Create a found poem! After reading the passage, go back and find the most important words and phrases. (You'll probably want to go back and read it a few times to make sure you have selected the exact ones you want. Remember that poetry contains only the most highly potent words to express a point.) Copy these words and phrases onto a sheet of paper (use large print, be neat, and spell everything correctly so that others will be able to read them when we share). Cut them apart. Arrange and rearrange them until they "speak" the message of the passage poetically. Paste them onto another sheet of paper, then display your poem.

Which assignment would *you* choose to do? Which would pique your interest more? Which would encourage you to do the multiple readings that are so important to understanding, especially for students who struggle? We suspect it's the latter.

When writing found poems, students can work together as they conduct the repeated readings and identify the key words and phrases. However, each student should be allowed to manipulate his or her own poem to make it personally meaningful.

Poetry Sources

If you are looking for poems that might inspire the poets in your classes—and you—these books will help:

Joyful Noise: Poems for Two Voices, by Paul Fleischman (Harper Trophy, 2004)

I Am Phoenix: Poems for Two Voices, by Paul Fleischman (Harper Trophy, 1989)

Wishes, Lies, and Dreams, by Kenneth Koch (Harper Paperbacks, 1999)

Rose, Where Did You Get That Red? by Kenneth Koch (Vintage Press, 1990)

Poetry from A to Z: A Guide for Young Writers, by Paul Janeczko (Simon & Schuster, 1994)

For the Love of Language: Poetry for Every Learner, by Nancy Cecil (Peguis, 1994)

■ Writing for and with Each Other

Writing for oneself as a way of thinking aloud on paper about learning has been the unifying thread of this chapter's activities. Yet every teacher knows that writers must also develop the ability to write effectively for a variety of audiences.

Roberta prompts her students to think about how to do this through an ungraded and unique activity (developed with her colleague Jen) based on *Bob the Builder*, a stop-motion animated children's program produced in the UK.

Roberta enters the classroom to the strains of *Bob the Builder*'s theme song. Curiosity piques, as students recognize the song and its spirit of working together. Roberta assigns partners, and each partner takes a turn working on a writing activity independently of the other.

In a brown paper lunch bag, each pair of students finds two baggies containing nine identical Legos and a lab paper (see Figure 4.1). Their task is to build an object out of the Legos and write clear directions about their process so that their partner will be able to construct the same object. Roberta scaffolds this activity before, during, and after:

Before

- Entry music captures students' attention and hints at the topic of the day.

- The lab sheet asks them to identify their prior knowledge and hypothesize about writing directions.

During

- Step-by-step directions guide their work.

- The writing is for an authentic audience and purpose.

- Language familiar to the writing process appears in words like *review* and *revise*.

- A potentially difficult word, *replicate*, is defined in context.

- Roberta circulates to help those who are having difficulty.

After

- Students receive immediate feedback about the clarity of their directions.

- They have an opportunity for self-assessment and peer assessment.

- The conclusions section invites metacognitive analysis and provides closure on the concept and the processes used.

- Students collaborate in creating this knowledge.

Students immediately see the results of writing that is unclear, incomplete, or just too sloppy when their partners are unable to replicate their Lego structure. The message hits home better than countless comments Roberta could write in red ink on their papers. Precise wording and neatness *do* count. Judging from student responses to *write one statement about how this activity will help you communicate with other science students,* they take important things away from this lesson. Following are typical examples.

Construction Worker: _____ Page # _____

YOU CAN DO IT!

PROBLEM: How do I write scientific directions well enough to allow other scientists to repeat my experimental process? (In this lab, every student will build an object and write directions to allow their lab partner to build an exact copy of it.)

BACKGROUND INFORMATION: (Jot down anything you know about writing directions.)

1. _____

2. _____

3. _____

4. _____

5. _____

HYPOTHESIS: (Answer the question in the problem, above, by using a complete sentence.)

_____

_____

EXPERIMENT:

1. You will write detailed directions on the next page for every step in your building process so that your partner can build an exact copy of your object.

2. Build an object using all of your blocks. You may not simply stack your blocks on top of each other. Build in all dimensions so that your object is a challenge for someone to replicate (to duplicate, copy, reproduce, or repeat).

3. Review and revise your directions to ensure that your lab partner will successfully replicate an exact copy of your object. (Extra credit will be given to you if your partner is successful.)

Figure 4.1. Writing for and with Each Other (*continues*)

4. My directions:

_____

_____

_____

_____

_____

_____

_____

_____

_____

_____

5. Hide your object in the brown paper bag. Be careful that it doesn't break.

6. Leave your directions on your lab desk.

7. Take the paper bag with your object in it with you.

8. Exchange seats with your partner.

9. Your partner will now try to replicate your object using your scientific directions.

10. When your partner is finished following your directions, rejoin your partner and compare the new object with your original model.

OBSERVATIONS:

1. Judge your lab partner's ability to replicate your object based on your directions by putting a check mark in the appropriate rating.

_____ PERFECT REPLICATION

_____ ALMOST PERFECT

_____ NOT SO HOT

_____ WHAT IS THAT??

Figure 4.1. *Continues*

2. Discuss your directions with your lab partner. What was clear about your writing? What was unclear? List them in the appropriate column.

CLEAR PARTS	UNCLEAR PARTS

CONCLUSIONS: Use complete sentences.

1. What was the point of this activity?

_____

_____

_____

2. How does scientific writing differ from writing in other classes?

_____

_____

_____

_____

3. Write one statement about how this activity will help you to communicate with other science students.

_____

_____

_____

Figure 4.1. *Continued*

- This activity will help me communicate with other students through writing because it taught me to be clear and thorough.

- It will teach us to speak clearly and calmly to other students.

- Scientific writing includes directions while most of language arts writing includes stories.

- It will teach us vocabulary words that will help us get our point across.

- This activity teaches me to be more specific.

- It helps you to work with a partner.

- It would help me understand their observing skills as well as mine.

- It gave me practice to work with another student to help them.

- It is a good way to try and make friends. You get to talk and communicate and get to know the person.

- You will know what you have to improve on in making directions.

- The activity helped us learn how to communicate by showing me that you have to include every detail.

- This activity helps us understand how they learn and interact with you.

- It helped me because I got to work with other students and got to know them better.

- Writing neatly will help me.

- It will help us understand each other and look at how other people think.

Important lessons for life in and out of school grow from this one activity. However, students also internalize important information about writing in science. In response to *How does scientific writing differ from writing in other classes?* typical comments include:

- This will help me think of others when I write an explanation, directions, or even just helping someone with an answer because you have to explain everything.

- It has to be very specific in order to be understood.

- Scientific writing is different because sometimes science needs to be in steps. Also, there are scientific words that have to be used in explanations.

- With scientific writing, you have to explain everything.

- You have more details than most other subjects.

- You have to say it clearly and neatly.

- You have to be exact.

- The difference is in scientific writing you explain how to do something in steps.

- Scientific writing differs from other class writing because in scientific writing you have to use bigger words.

Of course, there are always students whose pearls of wisdom provide us with a chuckle on the bad days when life is getting us down:

- In science we have to use special terms instead of just words.

- Scientific writing is true and others are false.

- You write about what you observe in scientific writing and what you are thinking in other subjects.

- Scientist has to write neat so that other scientists can read it.

But even here we see seeds of truth and know that they've taken away some new understandings about writing in science!

■ Writing Invites Learning

The writing we have proposed in this chapter invites learning. It invites reading. Most of all, it is a scaffold that invites everyone in, that gives every student the opportunity to participate and learn. Students use their newly learned vocabulary and content to make meaningful messages. We think it really counts—just not always for a grade.

CHAPTER

Many Paths, One Destination: Tapping into Different Learning Styles

We remember one teacher whose units all followed the same pattern: present the vocabulary list, read the textbook, outline the chapter, show a video, assign the questions at the end of the chapter, give a test. Next unit? Same pattern.

Although we believe in establishing routines so that students understand expectations, this is predictability run amok. Besides being boring, this pattern plays to the natural strengths of only some of the students—those who read well and prefer learning alone in a sequential structure. Students' learning styles and intelligences vary widely (Gregorc 1986; Gardner 1993). Teaching in just one way and offering learning opportunities in just one mode are being negligent. Varying the ways in which we approach subject matter—through dramatics, music, movement, and the visual arts—invites more students into learning and makes them eager to come to class.

■ Acting Out

Mention dramatics and many teachers shudder—building sets, designing costumes, conducting rehearsals, and overseeing ticket sales are a lot of work, never mind surviving opening-night jitters. We wholeheartedly support dramatic productions in our schools, but this is not what we are advocating here. The school play is an end product. What we are talking about is dramatics-as-process, a scaffold for reading and writing to understand. It draws on inter- and intrapersonal intelligences and opens a different door to learning.

Dealing with Unclear Text

In the textbook that Roberta uses, the section that explains changes of state is very confusing, even for the best readers. Acting out coupled with some writing, however, makes it clear.

When students enter class, Roberta asks them to open their books to the section on vaporization and read it. Then she displays the following jottings prompt and asks them to fill in the "before" section:

Denver Boil

Denver is called the "mile-high city." It has higher elevation and less atmospheric pressure than Oxford [the town in which Roberta teaches]. In Denver, water boils at a lower temperature than in Oxford. Explain why.

BEFORE:

AFTER:

In between the "before" and "after" sections, Roberta takes the class outside. She draws a huge kettle on the sidewalk with chalk (this could be done indoors with big paper if the weather isn't cooperating) and puts some of the students, playing water molecules, into it. She places other students, playing air molecules, above the pot of water. Then the students simulate what happens when water boils and its molecules escape into the atmosphere in Oxford (altitude 436 feet) and again in Denver (altitude 5280 feet).

After this brief dramatics-as-process activity, the students return to the classroom and think through their newfound understanding by completing the "after" section. Then they talk about their observations with another student.

In the class discussion that follows, Roberta is always pleased to see that students not only understand the content but also realize something about reading. Texts are not always written clearly. By comparing their "before" and "after" explanations, students see the importance of recognizing when something is not making sense and consulting another source for information.

The next day, Roberta brings in a brownie mix, reads the alternate directions on the back of the box for baking at high elevations, and asks the students to jot down an explanation. With visions of themselves as molecules dancing in their heads, they have no difficulty doing so!

Enlivening Boring Text Material

One of the dullest portions of the textbook Donna uses in her undergraduate classes is the section on the history of the English language. It is dense, full of facts and obsolete words. When text is dense and impenetrable, readers need a fix-up strategy. They are often told to reread it. Their reaction? "Ugh, it was bad enough the first time."

Dramatics to the rescue! Acting out brings forth a willingness to revisit the text. Donna breaks the text into four parts—Old English, Middle English, Modern English, and Contemporary Language Additions—has students count off by fours, and assigns each group to read one section three times:

1. First time: get an overview.

2. Second time: brainstorm ways to dramatize it.

3. Third time: come up with props that will aid your presentation.

At the next class meeting, students enter with tote bags containing tiaras, chocolate bars, capes, figurines, stuffed animals, anything they think connects in some way with their language era. Donna gives the groups twenty-five minutes to share their ideas for dramatizing their language period and conduct a brief rehearsal.

Then it's show time! Each skit takes less than five minutes and is hilarious. Students act out the Norman Conquest; borrowing words from other countries; the first printing press; and contemporary compounding. Laughter abounds. After each skit, Donna asks students to jot down notes on the memorable performances (*Jay was hysterical in the missionary nun's habit, a black garbage bag with a tin foil cross on it . . . they all fell down in the Great Vowel Shift . . . Jen used the overhead projector as a printing press*), attaching their classmates' names, props, and actions to the era. Before the midterm exam, she tells them to consult these notes when revisiting the text section dealing with each language period. Nearly everyone answers the questions on the history of the English language correctly.

Propping Up Current Events

A simple prop that hints at the essence of an incident can make a ho-hum current events report memorable. Dressing in a coat, hat, several scarves, mittens, and shivering a lot while reporting on the record-breaking temperatures in the Midwest captures the reality behind the numbers. A toy or paper airplane that takes off, then sputters and falls to the floor, summarizes an airplane crash. A folded blanket that gets handed to a fellow student pretending to be a homeless person celebrates the good deed of a local group collecting blankets for the needy. Attempting to drink from an empty water bottle illustrates the plight of those in a drought-stricken area.

Students can bring in their own props or scavenge through the prop box you keep loaded with yard sale finds and junk you no longer want. As with the previous activity, tell students to read the article three times—once for an overview, a second time to identify the major points to present, and a third time to think about a prop to accompany their report.

Sadly, the news is filled with reports of shootings, war, and other atrocities that involve weapons not suitable for school. In one school in which a student made a cardboard gun for his current events report, a teacher, from a distance, saw him walking into the building with what looked like a weapon. Minutes later, the police arrived. So be sure to preface your invitation into drama with a caveat about what is acceptable.

People, Places, and Things

Adding people, places, and things to our teaching opens still another channel of learning. Students remember their parts and those of their friends, the "stage" on which they played, and the props that provided extra cues. Those students with strong interpersonal intelligence shine in this type of activity—and they are often not those who shine when just using texts. Dramatics not only plays to their strength but also lets them model this intelligence for others. Moreover, it is active and playful, attributes important to learning and to life. Think about the texts you use. How might you use dramatics to bring them to life? Are there parts that are confusing? Boring? Are there speeches that students could act out rather than just read?

■ The Invitation of Music

While preparing for a chemistry lab about identifying elements by examining their physical characteristics, Roberta and her colleagues spontaneously break into the theme song from the TV show *CSI: Crime Scene Investigation*. After laughing self-consciously, they realize that they have stumbled on a good idea. Instead of calling the lab Experiment 1, they name it Who Are You? (Who, Who, Who, Who?) and play this song by The Who as students enter class on the day of the experiment. It turns out to be a very successful "before" activity: it draws students immediately into the lab, calls attention to the lab's purpose, and later helps students remember its procedures and conclusions.

Bolstered by this success, Roberta and her colleagues rename subsequent labs You Light Up My Life (creating complete circuits), Hot, Hot, Hot (using alcohol burners), Drip, Drip, Drip Goes the Water (a distillation lab), and Breaking Up Is Hard to Do (separating compounds into elements), each introduced by the appropriate song playing in the background. Roberta smiles when she hears students humming the theme song during critical parts of a lab, and singing "drip, drip, drip goes the water" as they watch distilled water falling from their glass tubing. When she can't think of the name for a lab, students volunteer song titles and bring in recordings of their favorite music to match what is going on in science class.

This can work in other content areas as well. On the day that Donna conducts a grammar review in her English class, she plays the Grammar Rock songs from the *Schoolhouse Rock!* cartoon series (Warburton 1973) as students enter the classroom. These twenty-somethings smile nostalgically, transported back to their childhood days, and often join in the refrains ("get your adverbs here" and "unpack your adjectives"). She also challenges them to write their own grammar songs to familiar tunes and asks them to bring in lyrics from their favorite songs. They analyze the grammar in the songs and rewrite them in Standard English. Singing these rewritten songs triggers laughter and a good discussion on audience and purpose for different grammars.

Resources for Teaching with Music

Google, YouTube, and TeacherTube are good Internet resources to explore when you're looking for a musical way to teach something that seems, at least at the moment, unteachable. When Roberta's students couldn't seem to understand the relationship between DNA and proteins, she surfed the Internet and stumbled onto "DNA Song," by Peter Weatherall (2008). This catchy (and maybe corny) tune reminds students of the connection, and to Roberta's surprise, they spontaneously join in on the refrain—*every* time in *every* class! They travel down the hall to their next class singing about DNA and how it contains the plan for everything inside us. The lesson sticks in a playful way, evidenced by great answers on the next test.

What possible musical connections are there to the subjects you teach? Some are naturals, like history, with its songs of war, patriotism, triumph, and despair: "The Erie Canal Song," "Follow the Drinking Gourd," "Dixie," "The Battle Hymn of the Republic," "Boogie Woogie Bugle Boy." Oh, how we envy our social studies colleagues! Other subjects, like science, require more creativity, but as you have seen, connections are possible.

We all have wonderful resources for identifying relevant music right in our schools. Any time we ask our music teacher colleagues, they are able to rattle off a list of songs for just about any topic we pose. And don't forget your students. As Roberta found, they are quite able to find the musical connections. Pop culture is their world, and frankly, those connections are the ones that are most likely to count in their learning.

Music invites us into our students' lives as well as inviting them into learning. We learn something else about who they are as human beings, their tastes and talents. It helps create empathy, a critical attribute for all of us.

■ Up and Moving

In science classrooms, students are often up and about, participating in labs. But not always. Some units do not include lab work and can easily become passive and teacher-directed. But middle school students need to move, and that urge can be harnessed in the interests of learning.

Station to Station

Preparing for a genetics unit, Roberta realizes that students will be working quietly and individually many days in a row. She decides to shake things up, and approaches her colleague Jen about redesigning this unit to involve movement and active learning. Together, the two of them plan a week of lessons based on cooperative groups in which students consult, learn, construct, and review together, over and over.

They organize the lessons as stations, each of which approaches the topic of genetics using a different type of activity. Rather than calling them station 1, station 2, and so on, they give each one an interesting name and print out the titles on large card stock that they hang from the ceiling above the related area (see Figure 5.1).

In advance, they strategically created student groups that included a mixture of abilities, aptitudes, and personalities that would work well together. They grouped together students who were reading well below grade level (and thus likely to "disappear" in a group of stronger readers) and planned to travel through the stations with them. They also arranged to have a bilingual volunteer parent or high school student or the English as a second language teacher on hand in each group in which a member needed English language learner support. The goal was

Figure 5.1. Station Identification

Station Name	Activity	Lesson	Differentiation
DNA Construction Zone	Model building	Students answer questions on a previously taught lesson about the structure of DNA. When deemed correct by the teacher, they "earn" a construction permit and kit to build a model of DNA. The kit consists of two types of pasta, four colors of precut pipe cleaners, and fishing line. Completed DNA models hang from the lights or ceiling as evidence of learning. Students complete a postconstruction worksheet.	The questions for the pre- and postbuilding activity can differ.
Vocabulary Playstation	Manipulating and playing with their vocabulary words	The packet consists of a crossword puzzle, word puzzles, concept maps, and magic squares to review their genetics vocabulary.	Word banks are included for the crossword puzzle and games. More examples are given, or particularly difficult answers are partially filled in.
Reading Corner	Magazine article	Students read a magazine article on genetics that contains newer information than found in their textbooks. They complete a guided reading activity together.	The magazine articles may differ. If using the same article, then the guided reading activity differs. Different types of questions, different vocabulary, and the variety of the responses required are varied.
DNA Dilemmas	Problem solving	Students solve four mysteries using prior knowledge and Punnett Squares.	The directions and examples are different.
Destination Station	Use of the Internet	The destination is a large screen computer or SMART Board that allows students to use a computer together to read about cloning and then participate in an animated cloning activity.	The guided reading or Web sites can be different.

Figure 5.2. Station-to-Station Genetics Lessons

for every student to feel he or she could contribute—no one would be relegated to copying others' work.

A change of routine, even one as energizing and exciting as this week was, can be unsettling. Therefore Roberta and Jen prepare their classes for the changes they would experience—the new room arrangement, the group assignments, and the nature of week:

- Entering the room each day, students find their group number and new station.

- Students are given two grades each day—an academic grade based on what they handed in and another for their contribution to the group.

- Behavior in the group is rated from 0 to 4 based on the following rubric:

    BEHAVIOR
    1. Follows all directions.
    2. Works to best of ability.
    3. Uses time wisely.
    4. Actively participates in station activities.
    5. Communicates well with others.

    RATING SCALE
    4   excellent
    3   good
    2   average
    1   needs a lot of improvement
    0   perfectly awful

The next day, students enter the classroom to find the furniture rearranged, signs hanging from the ceiling, and a classroom map on the board showing the location and name of each station. They consult the map, move to their assigned station, and open a folder (tailor-made for the group) containing their assignment and the directions they need to follow. At the end of the period, they tuck their work inside the folder and turn it in. Figure 5.2 shows the stations and how they can be adapted to meet individual needs.

Roberta and Jen concede that the preparation for this kind of activity is time-consuming and therefore much easier when done with a colleague. However, once the initial work is complete, day-to-day classes move very smoothly.

Station-to-station learning will not work for every topic in every subject, nor should it. However, when it fits with goals for a unit, it's a powerful way to get students moving and doing things together in an active, constructive way. With just a bit of brainstorming, we came up with these possibilities. Have fun brainstorming your own!

Subject	Topic	Activities
Geography	A destination (city, state, or country)	Preparation for a vacation: maps; travel arrangements; sites to see; culture; weather; food; politics
Math	Geometric figures	Practical uses; architectural uses; problem-solving activities; variations; drawing/drafting; formulas for area and volume
Health	Body systems	Models; drawings; body organs; diseases; vocabulary
History	Renaissance	Political maps; life of the common person; advances in medicine; new words and origins; leaders and ideas of the time in science, religion, the arts, government.
Poetry	American poets	Illustrate a poem; learn about famous poets; rewrite a poem in another style; use poems for different purposes; read poems aloud

Go to Your Corner

When the topic lends itself to students' having various choices or opinions, this activity will get them out of their seats, moving, and thinking. For one of Roberta's jottings (see Chapter 4) students have to identify and defend their choice of metaphor for a cell as either: (a) a building block, (b) a living organism, (c) a complex factory, or (d) all of the above. After students have completed the jotting, Roberta labels the corners of her classroom a, b, c, and d and tells students to go to the corner that corresponds to their answer. Each corner group talks together about their choice, solidifying their defense, before reporting to the whole class. Each answer is correct, depending upon how a cell is interpreted, so the conversation is spirited and wonderful thinking occurs.

You can use the classroom-corner technique to create groups for any discussion. Vary how you identify the corners: birth order (youngest children, middle children, oldest children, and only children) or birth months (January to March, April to June, July to September, and October to December), for example. Random criteria ensure that students talk to those with whom they normally do not and that new connections are made. The activity of moving, then standing—or sitting cross-legged on the floor—to talk provides a welcome change.

Corners of the room become sides of the room following a jotting in which Roberta asks, "Does ice cream have heat? Why or why not?" After students write their answers, they move to the two sides of the room, one side for yes, the other for no. A few volunteers read their reasons, then all are offered the chance to move to the other side if they have changed their mind. After crossing the room many times, the students arrive at the "aha": it's possible to measure the temperature of ice cream, and temperature measures the speed of molecular activity. Moving molecules generate heat; therefore ice cream has heat! Roberta praises them for their thinking and sharing. They return to their seats to revise their jottings if necessary.

Any conversation can be conducted as a whole class with students in their seats. But why not vary the pace and the energy level? It's good for everyone.

Ferris Wheel

Students seated at four-top tables or gathered in other groupings of four often turn and talk to their fellow group members, with whom they have established a comfortable rapport. A Ferris wheel technique can add some movement to this kind of sharing:

- Before a lecture, video, demonstration, or reading, alert students to get ready to note all the important information they will want to share with others.

- Afterward, give students a minute to review their notes and put the top three pieces of important information "in their head."

- Ask students to turn to a fresh page in their notebooks, then stand up behind their chairs.

- On a signal from you, have them move, Ferris wheel fashion, to the space or desk of the person next to them and write one of their top three ideas in that person's notebook.

- Continue the Ferris wheel motion, as students read the previous ideas written by their classmates and add a different one, until everyone has rotated back to her or his original position.

- Students read the ideas that others have written for them and add any additional ideas they were reminded of during the activity.

This is essentially a review, but the movement gets the blood circulating and keeps the mind active. It's very useful when many facts or ideas have been presented and can be used with any subject. Seeing what others have recalled adds to each student's total understanding. The writing task is simple, just a few words or phrases, so everyone is able to participate.

GOGO

GOGO is the acronym for a cooperative learning idea called Give One, Get One (Kagan 1992). Similar to the Ferris wheel, it allows students to get up out of their seats and share knowledge with their peers and is most often used to access prior knowledge. Students list what they know about a subject. Then they draw a line under their entries to separate their contributions from the ones they will now gather from others. Next, they move around the class, comparing lists, "giving" an idea to a classmate and "getting" one in return. This is a good "before" activity when students are likely to have a fair amount of prior knowledge about a topic, but we use it mainly as an "after" activity to sum up what students have learned.

The repetition of ideas, as students compare lists and see similarities, is valuable reexposure to both the content and language of the lesson. When differences surface, students have a chance to teach one another and sometimes to question whether their understanding is correct or not, which turns into a genuine reason for them to ask you for clarification. Certainly, you could attempt the same thing by stating, "To sum up, remember these points. . . . Any questions?" but the level of brain activity and commitment inherent in GOGO is much higher. The writing task is brief and accessible to all, giving everyone an opportunity to participate.

■ Visual Arts

As we've oft been told, a picture is worth a thousand words. The students in our classes do a lot of sketching (not to create works of art but to stretch the brain by designing and creating a new way to show information) and look at lots of pictures and cartoons. Graphic renderings are a conduit to learning for everyone but are especially important for those who have difficulty with language. Spatial intelligence, empathy, and meaning all come to life in a different way through the visual arts.

Foldables

Foldables, an idea developed and registered as a trademark by Dinah Zike (www.dinah.com), are sometimes called flip books. An easy way for students to actively construct and organize knowledge, they are still another way you can scaffold their understanding by having them use the elements of design and drawing to look at learning—and life—differently. Here's how to make one:

1. Take a piece of paper, short side at the top, and fold it in half lengthwise, from the right side to the left side.

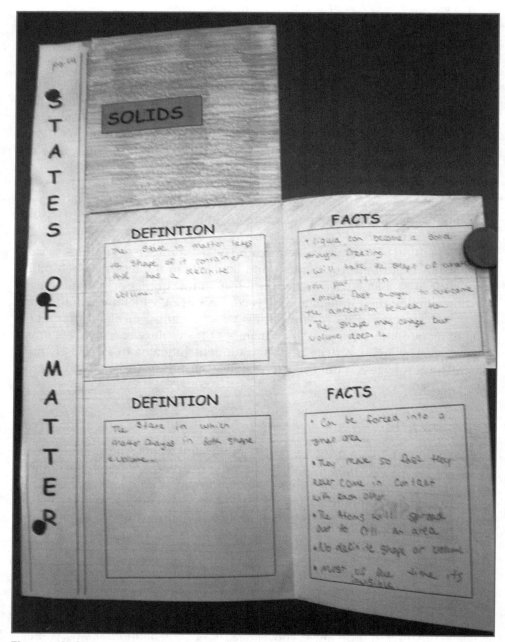

Figure 5.3. States of Matter Foldable

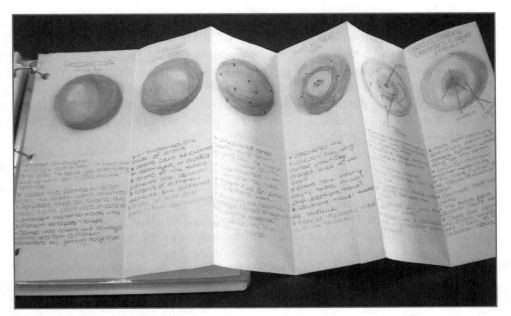

Figure 5.4. Time Line Foldable

2. Fold this double thickness into thirds, thus creating six segments, three on top of three. Unfold.

3. Using scissors, cut along two of the fold lines in the top thickness, from the outside edge to the centerfold, to create flaps that can flip up to reveal information written underneath.

Although many teachers have students create foldables on large sheets of paper suitable for display, Roberta has her students construct foldables that fit into the three-ring notebooks they use during labs, homework, and study sessions.

Foldable notes while reading. Roberta starts students out with a foldable on which they take notes while reading a section of their textbook on states of matter (see Figure 5.3). She distributes a foldable labeled *states of matter* vertically along the left side. The words *solids*, *liquids*, and *gases* appear when the handout is folded. Inside, there are boxes labeled *definition* and *facts*. Students make two cuts in the upper thickness of the fold so they can flip open each section. As they read, they jot their notes as a bulleted list, a skill that Roberta teaches by showing an example of her own before she asks them to do it alone. Later, students often color-code each state to differentiate them further. (Roberta has them complete a similar foldable when studying mixtures—solutions, suspensions, and colloids—varying the format with *definition* on the upper fold and *characteristics* and *examples* underneath.)

Vocabulary development foldables. With a slight variation, Roberta uses foldables for vocabulary development. The eleven key vocabulary words in her unit on matter fall into three basic categories: atomic structure, atomic particles, and atomic math. She lists the definitions in one column, keeping the words grouped by category, and provides a second column in which students write the words. They fold the paper along the line that divides the two columns and make cuts in the top fold to divide the words into the three categories. When they unfold each section, they see words that are related conceptually, and the students study the words together to discern similarities and differences.

Time line foldables. By combining three sheets of paper, Roberta creates accordion foldables that detail a time line for the development of atomic theory (see Figure 5.4). Students fold each of the three papers in half lengthwise, then glue them together side by side. This creates six columns that, when folded in half lengthwise once again, become twelve sections. Students draw the atom at different stages in history in the top of each section. Below that, they take notes on the development of atomic theory during that era. This becomes an easy and very effective way to show that science theory does change with advancements in technology. As a follow-up, Roberta shares a quote from an old copy of an encyclopedia and asks students to properly identify its place on their foldable time line.

Foldables categorizing information. Sarah, an eighth-grade teacher, has her students create foldables out of nine-by-eleven-inch construction paper, which she then displays on a wall in her classroom. The foldables categorize information, questions on the top flap, answers underneath. Because they try to create interesting and good-looking work, Sarah's students spend lots of time on the topic. And more work on the topic means assimilating more information that is more easily remembered during labs or tests.

The simpler the better. The point is not to make the construction of the foldables a complicated process, but to use them as a means to an end—learning the content. Teachers ask Roberta if foldables aren't perhaps too complicated for struggling students. To which she responds, "Au contraire!" The student in her class who had the most difficulty creating a foldable with six columns using three sheets of paper was a brilliant student, a talented athlete, and wonderful flutist. She just couldn't see how different sheets of paper could be connected to create the foldable. She needed a lot of help from her teacher and classmates, all the while retaining a good sense of humor about her lopsided construction! If someone has a physical problem with folding and applying glue, pair them with another student who is quick at such work or bring in an aide or volunteer to help. (Glue sticks are much easier to use than bottles or tubes of glue. No one wants to stick to the desks for the rest of the day!)

Possibilities/variations. Basic foldables work for any subject:

- *Vocabulary development.* One section for an illustration, one for the definition, one for use in a sentence.

- *Social studies.* Geography terms (*peninsula, isthmus, island, plateau*)—one section for a drawing, one for the definition, one for examples.

- *Math.* Geometric shapes—one section for a drawing, one for a definition, one for a practical example.

- *Literature.* Plot development—one section for the initiating event, one section for a rising action, one section for the climax (or initiating event, climax, and resolution).

Longer accordion foldables also work for any subject.

- *English.* Parts of speech, definitions, and examples.

- *Trigonometry.* Terms, definitions, and practical applications.

- *Social studies.* A travel brochure for a country highlighting its industries, major landmarks, culture, and so forth.

- *Literature.* Comparisons of authors.

- *Music.* Type of music, composers, representative songs.

- *Psychology.* Comparison of important figures in the field.

- *Health.* Body systems, definitions, functions, organs found in each.

Poster foldables also apply to any subject.

- *Test reviews.* Major categories on the flap, appropriate information underneath.

- *PowerPoint displays.* Major topics of a PowerPoint presentation on the flaps, students' notes underneath.

Photo Ops

Beverly Bimes-Michalak (1990) developed a warm-up writing technique in which students look at a picture of a person cut from a magazine and respond to prompts such as:

I've just come from . . .

Now I'm thinking . . .

One thing that I'm afraid of is . . .

What I'd like most to do is . . .

People say I am . . .

One question that I have is . . .

I'm happiest when . . .

I feel most important when . . .

I'm saddest when . . .

If I could have one wish, it would be to . . .

I like to be called . . .

In a workshop, Donna wrote about a magazine advertisement for an inanimate object, a washer, to show the flexibility of the prompts:

> I've just come from the appliance store. Now I'm thinking that I'll really have to work hard because these people have three active little children. One thing that I'm afraid of is that they'll play in the greasy garage and I won't be able to get the stains out of their clothes. What I'd like most to do is just wash things on my gentle cycle. People say I'm tough enough to handle any laundry challenge. One question that I have is, "Where did they get *that* information?" I'm happiest when I don't have to work so hard. I feel most important when I see the family dressed in clean, bright clothes that I've washed with little effort. I'm saddest when I wash and wash and wash, and still the stains don't come out. If I could have one wish, it would be to eliminate the dirt and grime from the world. I like to be called Easy Wash.

Who would think it possible to arouse empathy, a key life aptitude, about a washer or other inanimate object?

That's exactly what this activity asks students to do, to get inside the head of someone or something else and project thoughts and feelings. Think about your subject matter. What pictures could evoke responses about key concepts you want to develop? Perhaps each student gets a different picture. Or perhaps your textbook features a picture that says it all. Or perhaps there is a famous picture or painting that you could project for all to see, like Washington crossing the Delaware or JFK in deep thought. Or a picture depicting multiple points of view, such as the Nuremberg trials or the march on Selma. Or a not-so-famous-but-right-on-the-money picture. Or . . . you get the idea. Structure your prompts so that you invite thinking about key ideas, and your students will *want* to share what they've written—which equals more exposures and deeper understanding.

Chris, a technology education teacher, was inspired by the idea of using inanimate objects to deepen his students' thinking. Over the years, he tore out magazine pictures of various forms of technology—everything from a wheel to a computer motherboard. He thought about the key concepts that he tries to get across in his classes—that technology in some form has been around since the invention of the wheel, that it both solves and creates problems, that people often fear it when it first appears—then converted them into prompts:

I was invented because . . .

I solve problems by . . .

I create problems when I . . .

People fear me because . . .

I'm best used as . . .

These stems can lead students who may never have considered the benefits *and* problems created by new technologies to become more critical thinkers.

Signs of the Times

Much of today's environmental print is sadly in need of editing. Challenge students to develop their editorial eye by spotting signs, menus, church leaflets, and other documents in their out-of-school lives that contain grammatical, usage, or mechanical errors. Have them bring in the documents (or photographs of them), identify the error, and suggest the correction. Place them on a bulletin board headed Help! Editor Needed! It will amaze you how quickly the display will fill up.

You can also have students categorize the types and frequency of errors (comma usage, misspelling, improper abbreviation) or speculate on what may have caused them (letters fell down or were removed by vandals, the display character set ran out of letters or punctuation symbols, simple carelessness, typos). You might even consider a letter-writing campaign in which students contact local businesses to call the errors to their attention!

Thank Goodness for Clip Art

As you've examined some of the examples in this book, you'll have noticed that Roberta often puts a piece of clip art on things she shares with students. This is not just for decoration. Pictures are strong nonverbal cues that are especially important for students who have difficulty with reading or oral language. Pictures are another way to remember, a channel into the brain that enhances what is read and said.

The Internet offers ready access to all sorts of clip art, making it quite easy to give students this added advantage. Are you artistic, or at least good with stick figures? Your personal drawings add a deeper sense of connection. How about your students? Your request to use their renderings in future classes might be just the motivation they need to work really, really hard to understand a concept.

Color Cueing

Color is a powerful cueing technique. Black words parading relentlessly on a page can be overwhelming, overload the mental circuits, and cause readers to shut down. When Roberta first heard about color cueing, she thought it might be too babyish for her middle schoolers. But she tried it and saw the benefits firsthand.

Body systems. Preparing to dissect a frog, Roberta's students must become familiar with thirty-two specific terms identifying elements of a frog's body systems. Color makes the task of learning these terms manageable. Roberta gives students a diagram of a frog, accompanied by a glossary of terms. Students select a color for the elements of each system, shade in the corresponding areas on the frog diagram in the chosen colors, and highlight the related terms in those same colors.

Her students give convincing testimony about the effectiveness of this technique:

- I love this method because when we get a quiz on it I try to remember what the color of the word is and match it with the color of the body system.

- The visual helps me understand. The colors kinda click.

- I think that it helped me because the colors popped to help me remember the vocabulary words.

- Well, I think the diagram with vocabulary really helps, and the color makes it easier. I don't know why.

Corrections and reviews. Colored pencils abound in Roberta's classroom because she has all but banned the use of erasers when students correct their work. Instead, she asks them to make corrections in a different color. She finds that students often spend time studying what they already know rather than what was new to them or was misunderstood. The addition of color points out the difference, making study time more efficient.

The colored pencils also appear the day after students have completed graphic organizers related to a reading assignment or taken notes on a lecture. Their minds weigh all this new information equally. Before starting a new lesson, Roberta prompts them to highlight the key words and phrases in the previous day's notes. The key points stand out when they reread their notes to prepare for a quiz.

Using highlighters. Allyson is a college graduate and a successful marketing manager who deals with pages of data in her job. She always has a pack of colored highlighters with her, thanks to a tip she received from Adrian, her high school instrumental music teacher. When Allyson was a junior, she was diagnosed with attention-deficit disorder and a mild learning disability. As the music she was learning became more complex, she had difficulty discerning markings in the score that indicated mood, changes of tempo, accidentals, and key signature. Allyson knew what these markings meant, but they were coming too quickly, running together, causing confusion. Adrian suggested she put a colored mark at the bar line of a measure in which a change was coming, certain colors indicating certain kinds of changes. She has carried this skill with her into professional life, marking different types of data in different colors. She thanks this wonderful teacher for giving her a scaffold that has enabled her to be what she is capable of being.

Analogical Thinking Through Art

A little art goes a long way in helping students develop higher-level thinking skills. To tap into their students' analogical thinking, Roberta and her fellow science teacher Jen have developed the cell analogy project, in which students liken their understanding of cell structure to things in their real world (for example, the nucleus is like a brain because it controls and coordinates the activities of the whole cell in the same way that the brain controls and coordinates the activities of the body). The task and its requirements are presented in step-by-step instructions (see Figure 5.5). Roberta supports her struggling students by giving them a planning sheet she codeveloped with learning support teacher Carla (see Figure 5.6).

Students enjoy showing their understanding in this nontraditional way and find all-important personal connections with their lives in the process. The photo in Figure 5.7 shows how one student, a lover of Disney World, connected her lives in and out of school.

■ Many Ways to Know and Show

There are many ways to know and many ways to show you know it. Learning is richer for all students when we vary the way we present our instruction. The aptitudes that students develop along the way prepare them for life in a more complex world. Learning—and teaching—this way is more fun.

CELL ANALOGY PROJECT

An analogy is _____

_____

PROJECT CHECKLIST: After you complete each section of this list, place a check mark next to the number. This will help you be sure to meet each requirement.

1. Draw an ANIMAL or PLANT cell on $8\frac{1}{2}$ by 11-inch paper. You can use computer paper or construction paper. You MUST include the following organelles:

   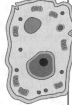

   1. Cell membrane
   2. Cytoplasm
   3. Nucleus
   4. Vacuole
   5. Mitochondria
   6. Choose **two** additional organelles and add them to your drawing.
   7. **EXTRA CREDIT:** ***"You can add up to two **more** organelles WITH analogies for extra credit"***

   > You will have 7-9 organelles WITH analogies.

2. Paste your cell drawing in the middle of a **poster**-sized piece of paper.

3. Title your poster by correctly identifying your cell as an animal or plant cell.

4. Neatly label each organelle.

5. Find the **function** (main job) of each organelle by reading your textbook, reviewing your notebook, or checking your glossary.

6. Find magazine pictures, newspaper photos, clip art, or original drawings of everyday items whose function you can **compare to the function** of each cell part.

7. Paste the pictures of everyday objects neatly around your cell drawing on the poster paper.

8. Draw a **neat** line from your everyday object to its matching cell part in your cell drawing. **You must use a ruler!**

9. Write an analogy neatly next to the picture of the everyday object to compare its function with the function of the cell part. Be sure to EXPLAIN the reasoning behind your analogies.

   EXAMPLE: You CANNOT use this analogy in your project:
   The nucleus is like a brain because it controls and coordinates the activities of the whole cell in the same way that the brain controls and coordinates the activities of the body.

10. Use LOTS OF COLOR! No pencil allowed on a poster. You may use colored markers, bright poster paper, construction paper accents, glitter, and/or puffy paint. BE CREATIVE!!

YOU WILL BE GRADED ON THE **NEATNESS, ACCURACY, AND COMPLETENESS** OF YOUR WORK. **MY PROJECT IS DUE ON** _____.

Figure 5.5. Step-by-Step Instructions for Cell Analogy Project

CREATE CELL ANALOGIES

1. The cell membrane is like _____ because it

_____

in the same way that _____

_____

2. The cytoplasm is like _____ because it

_____

in the same way that _____

_____

3. The nucleus is like _____ because it

_____

in the same way that _____

_____

4. The mitochondria is like _____ because it

_____

in the same way that _____

_____

5. The _____ is like _____ because it

_____

in the same way that _____

_____

6. The_____ is like _____ because it

_____

in the same way that _____

_____

EXTRA CREDIT:

7. The nucleus is like _____ because it

_____

in the same way that _____

_____

8. The nucleus is like _____ because it

_____

in the same way that _____

_____

Figure 5.6. Differentiated Instructions for Cell Analogy Project.

Figure 5.7. Completed Cell Analogy Project

CHAPTER

Who Is Responsible for Students' Learning?

While walking down the hall in a school that shall be nameless, we overheard:

> I am not going to read the text to you; I am not Mother Goose! *You* are responsible for your own learning, *not me*. Take it home and read it on you own, and you can expect a test tomorrow.

It was all we could do to keep from running into that classroom and shaking the teacher while saying emphatically, "Their learning *is* your responsibility! That's why you are called a *teacher*, not a camp counselor, entertainer, or babysitter!" This book was born out of our strong sense of our responsibility as teachers to help all students learn.

■ Getting Everyone Off to a Good Start

Taking responsibility for establishing an environment in which everyone can learn begins on the first day of school. Put yourself in a student's place. You enter the classroom wondering, "Who is this teacher? What's she like? What's this course about? What will I have to do? Will I get it? Will I feel comfortable here?" Of course, some students enter smugly, bolstered by their track record of good grades: "Another year, more success." Others enter fearfully, convinced that learning here will not come easily because it hasn't in the past: "Another year, more evidence that I can't." Some enter apathetically, daring us to make learning meaningful: "Another year, ho-hum."

We enter zealously. There is so much to cover—the rules, the procedures, the course of study, the schedule. We plunge in, eager to get through the beginning-of-the-year dos and don'ts, explanations, rules, and procedures so we can get to the real meat of the course—the content. In the process, we inadvertently can establish an environment that is off-putting and frightening for students to whom learning has not come easily or who have not always had the best school success.

Advice on how to start the school year abounds, some of it "teacher lore" that has been passed down over generations. Early in our careers, an experienced colleague offered this bit of advice: "Don't smile until Christmas." Hidden in this cryptic statement was a message. *Don't let them walk all over you. Establish yourself as the martinet, the order keeper. Control them by making them fear you.* Clearly, this teacher knew that productive teaching and learning cannot take place in chaos, but the underlying mind-set spoke of an adversarial relationship. Is this the kind of environment that welcomes learners?

Current advice about starting the school year, fortunately, is much more collaborative and proactive. Charlotte Danielson (2007) tells us that

> a smoothly functioning classroom is a prerequisite to good instruction. The best instructional techniques are worthless in a chaotic environment. Therefore, teachers find that they must develop procedures for the smooth operation of the classroom and the efficient use of time before they can focus on instructional techniques. One of the marks of expert teachers is that they take the time required to establish their routines and procedures at the onset of the school year. . . . In a well-managed classroom, procedures and transitions are seamless, and students assume responsibility of the classroom's smooth operation. (69–70)

Between the first day of school and students' assumption of responsibility for the smooth operation of the classroom stands the teacher who paves the way. As our mothers told us, first impressions count. How can we set the stage for success, welcoming and engaging them all, right from the start?

Pillars of Personal Responsibility

Over the years, teachers have developed classroom rules alone and in collaboration with their classes, posting them prominently as a reminder to all about expectations. The problem with a set of rules, regardless of who has developed them, is that they are not finite. Just when you feel you've covered all the bases, a new situation arises. So you add still another rule to the chart. Then it happens again . . . and again . . . and soon, the list of rules covers the entire wall, far too many for anyone to remember.

Rather than a set of rules, consider the habits of mind that are basic to all human behavior. We call these the *pillars of personal responsibility*. These habits of mind—*respect, learning,* and *health and safety*—are essential both in and beyond the classroom. As an alternative to a growing list of classroom rules, picture three long sheets of butcher paper, simulating three pillars (even decorated at the top with pillarlike scrollwork if you have an artistic bent), hanging in the classroom. At the top of the first pillar is:

We will do things that show
RESPECT
for ourselves and others.

At the top of the second pillar is:

We will do things that promote
LEARNING
in ourselves and others.

And on the third pillar we see:

We will do things that promote
HEALTH and SAFETY
in ourselves and others.

What is more basic—and easier to remember—than these three statements? All of the potential "rules" merely support them. Why can't we interrupt a speaker or pick on others? Because it is disrespectful. Why can't we sharpen our pencils in the middle of class, refuse to contribute to discussions, or skip homework assignments? Because these things interfere with our own or our classmates' learning. Why can't we chew gum, lean our chairs on their two back legs, or keep our backpacks in the aisle? Because these actions affect our health and safety.

Use the rest of each pillar to develop specific examples and nonexamples. Under the headings, draw a T-chart with "looks like" on one side and "does not look like" on the other. Find out what your students know about classroom expectations by having them suggest examples for each column:

We will do things that promote

LEARNING
in ourselves and others.

Looks like . . .	*Does not look like . . .*
Sharpening pencils before class	Interrupting class to sharpen pencils
Completing homework	Blowing off homework
Coming to class on time	Being late
Paying attention	Daydreaming
Etc.	Etc.

As the year progresses, catch students "being good," doing things that "look like" the three pillars. Add them to the list. Of course, behavior will not always be as it should. When it isn't, refer to the three pillars and discuss what happened. Add it to the "does not look like" list. Over time, the examples and nonexamples listed on the three basic pillars of behavior will not only develop proper behavior for your class but also anchor habits that are good for life. Within this kind of ethos, all students feel that learning is safe.

Classroom Procedures

Contrary to the early career advice she was given, Roberta does smile as she lays the groundwork for building community within her classroom. Her overview of procedures and expectations takes on a bit of life when she has her students co-create them.

She begins by giving students a worksheet with fill-in-the-blank spaces that hint at expectations and procedures in her class (see Figure 6.1). Then they brainstorm, drawing on their prior knowledge about behavior and grading schemes. As they agree on answers, she takes notes on her SMART Board copy of the same worksheet. Class discussion is lively and inclusive as students see that she listens and is fair. Eventually, a student always recognizes the twist she has embedded in the list of positive behavior. The first letter of each spells out her last name! As they work through the paper, they learn that there will be no surprises about grading, and that the course of study promises the excitement of experiments and active learning. Roberta expects parents to sign this paper as well, and this becomes her first homework assignment of the year.

Throughout this simple activity, everyone has a chance to participate, and everyone's opinion and ideas count. These are key points Roberta wants to make right from the start. She emphasizes the importance of respect, because respect for self and others is at the heart of everything else. She respects her students and expects their respect in return. This is a mantra to which she will return again and again as the year goes on, continuing to give and seek examples of what it looks like, sounds like, and feels like.

Group Work

Group work is a big part of Roberta's classes. Lab partnerships, discussion groups, and problem-solving teams all require that students work collaboratively and cooperatively. She had a very frustrating year when she first taught a class that had a large number of students labeled learning disabled and English language learners. From the beginning of the year, she had provided careful scaffolding to help them read their textbook for understanding and was pleased with the results. Labels aside, they were being successful, comfortable students. She was sure this would automatically carry over into group work. And knowing that teens are social animals, she was sure they would love it.

CLASSROOM PROCEDURES

Make sure that you are _in your seat on time_ .
Contribute by _raising a silent hand_ .
Missed work _must be made up_ .
Always be _prepared_ — Bring your covered
text book , _agenda_ , _notebook_ ,
AR book , and _2 pencils_ .
Never _touch_ anything in the room.
Use the _pencil sharpener_ and _lavatory_ at the
beginning/end of the period.
Show _respect_ for everyone!

GRADING

Grading is done on a _point basis_ .
Grade = _points earned ÷ total possible points = %_
Grading is based on:

a. _Homework_
b. _Quizzes - surprise_
c. _Tests - announced_
d. _Participation_
e. _Class work + Labs_
f. _Note book_

COURSE OF STUDY

1. Scientific Method
2. Microscope and Cells
3. Genetics
4. Natural Selection
5. Chemistry
6. Classification

I have read and discussed this information with my child.

_____   _____
Parent signature   Parent printed name

Figure 6.1. Classroom Procedures

What a surprise! When Roberta asked students to break into groups to discuss topics and perform tasks together, the labeled students became very resistant. Past roles and old insecurities emerged. School-savvy students overtook the groups, dominating the discussions and ignoring everyone else. Labeled students retreated, refusing to take part, turning their attention to nonschool distractions.

Roberta learned that she had to address the concept of group work and individual responsibility at the beginning of the year, not leave it to chance. She had to harness students' social nature and help them shape it into acceptable learning behavior.

Since then, she addresses group work on day two. Because time is always at a premium, she combines this exercise in working together with a key task from her curriculum—defining the word *science*. To keep the pace varied and the learning experience lively, she combines three teaching strategies—T-charts, group roles, and dot voting.

T-charts. Before breaking students into groups, Roberta focuses on behavior and expectations. She displays a T-chart headed with a picture of an eye (*what I will see*) and an ear (*what I will hear*). Drawing on their prior knowledge and their common sense, her students brainstorm appropriate stances and behavior under each. Under the eye, students list such ideas as *heads close together, students facing each other, pencils moving, no looking out windows, students in their seats.* Under the ear, their suggestions include *science words, no talking about sports or lunch or TV, inside six-inch voices, respectful comments, listen to everybody's idea.* Roberta lists their ideas and praises them for their innate understanding of the task ahead. She also editorializes on their ideas, explaining the "why" of each of their suggestions and providing suggestions of her own.

Group roles. She then has students count off to form random groups of four and presents the task: *define science.* She gives each group a sheet of construction paper and a marker, and explains that every member of the group will have an individual role to play. They giggle with her when she describes herself as the "supreme (but very benevolent) dictator" who assigns these jobs.

- One student will be the *leader*, who will lead (not dominate) the discussion and keep an eye on the clock to be sure the task is finished in the time allotted.

- Another student will be the *recorder*, responsible for writing the definition on the paper (and assuring that the marker is not misused).

- A third group member will be the *reporter*, who will read and explain the group's work to the entire class.

- Finally, one student will function as an *observer*, who will monitor the group's interactions and adherence to the rules on the T-chart, now posted prominently in the classroom.

The group members put their heads together and when each group has settled on a definition of science, the recorders display the definitions on the board and the reporters share their group's work.

Dot voting. At this point, it's time to get everyone thinking. Roberta gives each student a sticky colored dot (available at office supply stores). She asks students to consider each definition carefully, then go to the board and affix their dot to the definition of science they think is most complete. She reassures them that all definitions at this point are best guesses and that they will be refining their ideas about science as time goes on. The definitions receiving the most stickers will remain on display. Responses garnering the most votes typically say things like:

- Science is the study of the world around us. How things work, different species, diseases, and inventions.

- Science is research, analysis, hypothesis, and it's also chemistry.

- Science is the study of why and how things happen in the world.

- Science is experimenting, nature, lab work, observing, hands-on work, chemistry, plant cells, scientific method, hypothesis, elements, research, data, analysis.

Roberta then gives students an operating definition of science—*science is knowledge about the world gained from observations and experiments*—and shows how this broad definition contains all their best guesses. She tells them that unlike in other fields, where 2 + 2 = 4 (in base ten) and the Battle of Hastings was fought in 1066, science is ever evolving as hypotheses are formed, tested, and evaluated.

As new scientific information unfolds in subsequent classes, Roberta revisits the definitions and helps students fold in new learning. The message embedded here is that learning is continual as we take what we know, revise it, and reach for more complete understanding. And with one another's help, we all learn more. With expectations set, these learners will be able to work together to everyone's advantage.

■ Working Together Productively

The teacher's responsibility does not begin and end with saying, "Get in groups and. . . ." We must be deliberate about how we group and for what purpose.

Turning and Talking

It is sometimes most appropriate for students to work in pairs. Turning and talking to a partner is a useful technique for inserting short breaks into a lecture, demonstration, or video during which students can process the information. You might ask students to:

- Recall key facts.

- Restate the information just presented in their own words.

- Sum up.

- Answer a question.

- Pose a question.

- Share an example.

- Relate a short experience.

- Brainstorm possible reasons.

- Make a best guess.

The intention of turning and talking is to maintain focus, keep everyone involved. The time spent is brief—often just thirty seconds to a minute—but long enough to make sure that students are engaged (or become reengaged) with what is happening in the class. Because students will often talk to the same person, vary the types of turn-and-talk partnering, some of which are discussed below.

Elbow buddies. As the name suggests, the person who sits beside you—at your elbow.

Compass buddies. Label the walls in your classroom with a geographic direction—north, south, east, west. (Borrow a compass from a science teacher colleague to identify the true directions if you aren't sure.) Students turn and talk to a north/south buddy or an east/west buddy. After a bit of experience, the pairings can get more complicated: northeast/southwest and northwest/southeast. Bonus feature: Students get practice with directions, for which your social studies colleagues will thank you.

Odd/even buddies. If your students sit in groups of four, assign each group member a number from one to four. When it is time to turn and talk, they do so as either odd buddies (numbers one and three) or even buddies (two and four).

Working in Larger Groups

Larger groups come into play when responses or interactions require longer periods of time. For example:

- more complex restatements

- larger amounts of information

- discussions

- confusion resolution

- projects

- problem solving

- collaborative writing

- debates

- defense of a position

Small groups are most useful when a task will benefit from the contributions of a number of people. In whole-class discussions, it is easy for students to hide if they choose, becoming invisible while others participate. And too often, students who struggle most take this option. In a small group, these students can contribute with a feeling of safety.

There are many ways to create groups. Which grouping pattern you choose depends on your purpose. Is it important that students are heterogeneously grouped? Homogeneously grouped? That certain students are together or separated? Or doesn't it matter?

Random groups. In some situations, group composition doesn't matter. When you want to create equal-size groups, counting off fills the bill. Determine what size groups you want and divide that number into your total class size. For example, if you want groups of four and you have twenty-eight students, have students count off by sevens. This will yield seven groups of four students each. If the size of the groups can be approximate, the following criteria will work:

- birth month

- birth order (oldest child, middle child, youngest child, only child)

- astrological sign

- number of siblings

- color of clothing worn that day

- first pets (dogs, cats, birds, hamsters, etc.)

- favorite sport teams

- school activities they participate in

Student-chosen partners. Students like to work with their friends, and when they stay on task, student-chosen pairs are a motivating and comfortable way to learn. Roberta uses sign-up sheets so students know she is aware of the groupings. Students sign up to work with four different partners—A, B, C, and D—in pairs that are often identified by a pun appropriate for the unit of study (Figure 6.2 is a group sign-up sheet for a cell unit). In other units, students "share viruses" (a unit

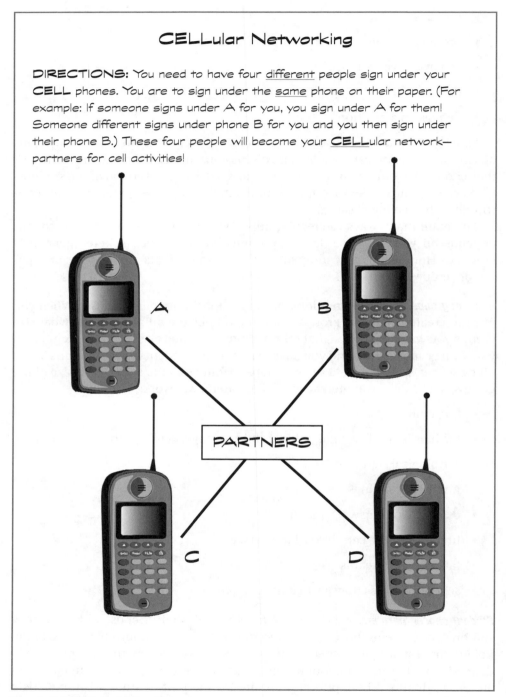

Figure 6.2. Cellular Networking

on diseases) and form "chemical bonds" (a chemistry unit). These are the people with whom they agree to learn and interact throughout the unit.

When Roberta wants to pair students with different partners for different activities, she can say, "Get with your A [or B or C or D] partner." In the chemistry unit, for example, students work with their A partner during a lab, their B partner when they assess a video, their C partner when they take shared notes, and their D partner when they complete a reading guide.

Clock buddies. Sometimes group composition has specific parameters. You may want to have a mix of ability or performance levels. Or you may want to have students of similar abilities work together so you can support or enrich them appropriately. And sometimes you want to avoid certain behavioral or personality combinations so that peace reigns in your classroom. Fourth-grade teacher Kevin Allen uses a strategy he calls "clock buddies" in these situations. It is a way for the teacher to set up different groupings to be used over a longer period of time.

First, draw a clock face with the twelve, three, six, and nine o'clock hours shown; provide a space for a student's name beside each time (see Figure 6.3). Duplicate these sheets so there is one for each student. Then, as the teacher, fill in the names for the twelve, six, and nine o'clock positions, with each of the four hours representing a different kind of partnering. Leave the three o'clock position blank so that students can choose a friend as a partner. For example:

12:00—a student who is approximately at the same ability or performance level

3:00—a classmate the student has chosen as someone with whom he or she would like to work

6:00—a student who is not at the same ability or performance level

9:00—a student who is a behavioral or personality match

When you want students of equal ability to work together, either to challenge the more capable or provide a scaffold for those who struggle, pair them with their twelve o'clock buddy. If you want students to benefit from a high/low-ability pairing, have them work with their six o'clock buddy. When you need to ensure that behavior or personality conflicts will not interfere with the work, assign nine o'clock buddies. When anything goes, allow them to work with their three o'clock buddy. Only you need to know what the time positions indicate. And you can change the names on the clocks as the year progresses and you learn more about your students and their needs.

Roll of the die. This is a variation on Kagan's (1992) numbered heads technique and is adaptable to any grouping pattern. Have students in each group count off, so that each has a number. Assign a task such as:

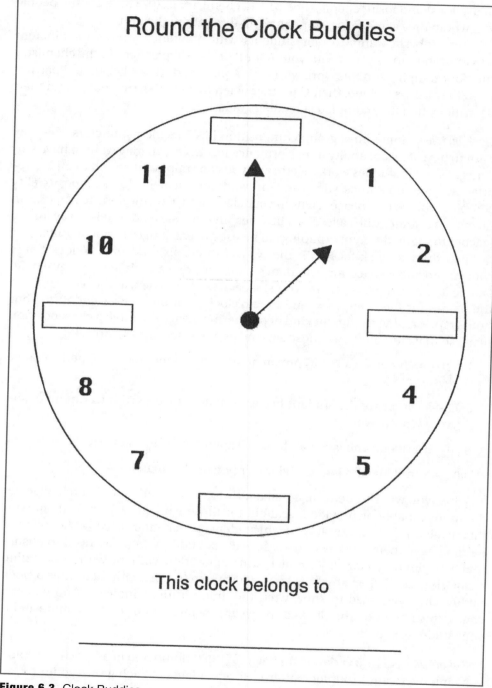

Figure 6.3. Clock Buddies

- Summarize information just presented.

- Explain how to do something.

- Review a concept.

- Brainstorm ideas.

Give the groups one to three minutes to complete the task; stress that every member of the group must be prepared to report the group's findings to the class. Then, roll a die to determine which group member reports.

With four-person groups, a roll of one through four identifies the reporter. If you roll a five, the group gets to decide which student will report. A roll of six means it's your turn as the teacher to complete the task. This technique is a good way to focus students' attention and a comfortable way to include all learners. Those who have more difficulty benefit from the explanations and ideas of stronger group members. Stronger group members benefit from clarifying or extending their thinking.

Dotted roles. This can also be used with any grouping pattern. Give each group an index card with four different-colored dots on it but with no explanation of what the dots mean. Each student then signs his or her name next to a different dot. Next, post the following duties:

> red dot—team leader (keeps everyone on task, manages time)
>
> blue dot—recorder (takes notes and organizes them, prints neatly)
>
> green dot—reporter (presents the team's ideas to the class)
>
> orange dot—observer (reports back to the team on their group dynamics— how did they do?)

For groups of more than four students, add purple dots, one for each additional member:

> purple dot—EXTRA! (Be a great team member who makes meaningful contributions!)

Speed dating. Speed dating is a social networking service in which single people in search of the perfect match have three minutes to tell a potential partner about themselves before a bell rings and they move on to meet the next person. The classroom version matches students with information and ideas. The technique works well for reviewing information before an exam or finding out what students already know about a topic.

Have students form equal outer and inner circles, facing one another. To begin, inner circle members have one minute (more or less, your call) to tell the people they are facing all the related facts or ideas they can think of. At the end of the allotted time, the students in the outer circle do the same, adding to the knowledge or ideas already presented. At the end of another timed segment, the inner circle students move clockwise to the next person, and the exchange process is repeated. As students move from person to person, information and ideas will invariably be repeated, which is good reinforcement. But with each successive movement of the circle, students will gain new insights as well.

■ Who "Gets It"? Who Doesn't?

If we only taught five students at a time, we would know with reasonable certainty how all of them were doing all the time, know who needed individual help when, and have the time and resources to provide it. Unfortunately, a class that size is pure fantasy. Teaching a real class, these things are very difficult to accomplish.

Let the Students Tell You

Personal response systems and electronic whiteboards can help, but they are expensive and many schools can't afford them. Fortunately, there are a number of "every student response" techniques that are inexpensive and simple to implement.

Cup monitoring. Kevin Bower, a sixth-grade teacher, uses a variation of Popham's (2008) traffic signals to let students know that it's normal to question whether you understand and to admit that you need help. Indeed, regularly monitoring one's understanding is the mark of a successful student.

Kevin gives each student three plastic cups, a green one, a yellow one, and a red one.

- Green means, "I understand."

- Yellow indicates some concern. "I think I'm okay, but I may need some help."

- Red means, "Help! I don't get this at all."

Students begin a lesson or reading assignment by stacking their cups, green one on top. As the lesson or reading proceeds, they restack the cups in accordance with their understanding. Kevin watches for the color changes and offers help immediately. He also stops from time to time and asks whether students understand a particular point, having them reposition their cups as necessary. Periodically, he asks students displaying green cups to explain or restate, knowing that it is easy to "hide" behind a green cup even if you don't understand.

Obviously, this technique must be based in trust and mutual respect. Students need to know that an admission that they need help will not be met with ridicule or impatience but that they will be praised for monitoring their understanding.

Close to the vest. Chances are, you've been in groups where the presenter asked everyone to signal understanding, agreement, or choice with thumbs up or thumbs down. And you've probably done what your students do—looked around and made the sign everyone else was making! This technique attempts to check this tendency. Instead of holding thumbs in the air for all to see, tell students to signal thumbs up or down "close to the vest"—right in front of their chests where you can see their response easily, but no one else can.

Signal cards. Having each student wield a trio of colored index cards also helps you monitor their learning. As with the plastic cups, green, yellow, and red indicate their level of understanding. Stop periodically in your lesson and ask them to raise the card appropriate to their assessment of their learning so far. If you see a number of yellow or red cards, you need to reexplain.

If the cards are colored on one side and white on the other, students' responses will be for your eyes only. They can keep them face down, white side up, on their desk until it is time to display them. (Have them code a tiny *g*, *y*, or *r* in the lower left-hand corner of the white side.)

A quartet or quintet of index cards, each with a letter of a predetermined word (preferably one that matches your course content, such as MATH or HIST, or the name of your school's mascot, for example), is another way to check for understanding. For example, "Hold up *M* if you think the answer is such-and-such, *A* if you think the answer is thus-and-so," and so on. Or you can accomplish the same thing with shapes: "Hold up your square for true, your triangle for false." Again, students can write the letter or shape on the back of each card so they know which is which.

The question hat. Many students, particularly those who struggle, are reluctant to ask for help; they don't want to appear different or needy. Even in a safe environment, asking a question in public can be unsettling. Find an old or unusual hat (think the Hogwarts School's Sorting Hat in the Harry Potter books) and ceremoniously name it the Question Hat. Put the hat in an easy-to-reach spot, perhaps on the corner of your desk, and tell students that whenever they have a question, need help, or are confused about the subject matter, they can jot their question on a slip of paper and place it in the hat. They do not need to sign their name unless they would like to speak with you privately.

Check the hat after each class and review or reexplain material as needed. Arrange to meet one-on-one with students who have signed their names. Before an exam, you might give everyone an identical slip of paper on which they either can ask a question about something that is confusing or simply say, "I don't have any questions right now." Asking everyone to write something, even if they don't have a question, removes the stigma; no one can tell who doesn't understand.

Refocus Attention

It happens to us all. The lesson is going along and our attention strays, or we begin a conversation with the person next to us, or we doodle on our notepads. Students who have difficulty are even more prone to this behavior, escaping to safer or more comfortable places when the going gets tough. Sixth-grade teacher Kevin, who is an avocational percussionist, uses a series of rhythmic signals to refocus his students' attention when he sees that it has strayed. Here are his cue words and what they signify:

hand = clap hands one time

table = slap hands on table one time

feet = stomp feet one time

twirl = circle hand in air while saying, "Whoooo!"

When Kevin notices off-task behavior, he quietly states a pattern, and the students closest to him execute the actions. The rest of the class listens for Kevin to call the next pattern so they can participate. By the time he calls the third pattern, which ends with "twirl," he has the entire class's attention. It might play out like this:

hands, hands, table, table. (A few students perform the pattern.)

hands, hands, table, table, feet, feet, hands. (More students join in.)

hands, table, feet, table, feet, feet, twirl. (Everyone is involved, and they end with a "Whoooo!")

Kevin never raises his voice. He doesn't flip the lights on and off, treating his students like young children. He doesn't threaten them with detention. He doesn't have to. Students get caught up in the rhythm. By the final "twirl," they are all smiles and ready to refocus and get back to work.

Differentiate Tasks

Roberta differentiates her reading guides, worksheets, and exams, tailoring them to the needs and levels of each class. She adds more complex items for stronger students, and gives fewer, simpler items to those who struggle. She builds in the right number of hints or other scaffolds for those needing help. Often, she ends up with three different versions of the same assignment—an organizational nightmare when multiplied by the many lessons she teaches.

She has devised a simple system for keeping track. She positions the clip art she places on her assignments (as described in Chapter 5) on the page according to the type of student—at the top for students who need little scaffolding, in the margin for average students, and at the bottom for those needing help. No one has ever asked why the clip art is positioned differently (if they began to suspect that it meant high, middle, low, she would change the positioning), and she can tell at a glance which paper is meant for which students.

Find Helping Hands

No matter how hard we try to provide for everyone's needs, the reality is that in today's diverse and inclusive classrooms, there simply are some students whose needs we have difficulty meeting. They require more personal attention than we can give without hindering the learning and behavior of the other students in the class. If we are fortunate, our schools provide us with classroom aides, but that is not always the case. Here are several ways you can welcome others into your classroom to help share the responsibility:

1. Talk to your principal about creative ways of scheduling faculty duties.

   • Perhaps there are teachers in your school who would prefer to help out in someone else's classroom rather than supervise the lunchroom or study hall.

   • Perhaps your school's special education teachers, English as a second language teachers, or reading specialists can build time into their schedules for in-class work.

   • Your school administrators themselves may be itching to have time away from the grind of administrivia and welcome an opportunity to work with a student.

2. Use the community as a resource.

   • If your school district has an educational foundation, contact someone on the staff. Groups like this often provide volunteer mentor tutors who work with individual students. They often also disperse funds you can use to pay a nominal stipend to tutors or at least host a very nice luncheon at the end of the year to thank them publicly.

   • Welcome senior citizens into the school. America's aging population and its many retirement communities are a rich resource of people with wisdom, experience, and patience waiting to be tapped. Some school districts even offer tax breaks to seniors who volunteer in the schools. The intergenerational understanding that accrues when students who need help are paired with people who have seen so much of life is an additional bonus.

   • Develop a network of retired teachers. They best know the challenges you face in meeting students' needs. They may no longer want a classroom of their own, but spending an hour or two a day helping one of your neediest students might be just the postcareer connection they seek.

- Rethink homeroom mothers and fathers. Many parents are actively involved in elementary classrooms, but once their children are in middle and high school, they keep a low profile. This often happens because their children believe having a parent in their school spells social disaster. Although their presence in their own children's classrooms might not be as appropriate in middle and high school, parents may still be interested in helping students in a different grade or a different class.

3. Use students as resources.

- Is there a college or university in your area? Education majors may be eager to build their resumes by working with students in real schools.

- High school students looking to fulfill their community service graduation requirement or broaden their college application profile may wish to work with students in younger grades. Future teachers clubs and organizations are promising leads as well.

- Pairing students with the same native language, whether in the same class or not, can be very effective in helping English language learners translate content and navigate their new school.

■ Research Your Own Teaching

How are students in our school district doing? What do they need? These two questions preoccupy the minds of teachers, administrators, school board members, and the general public. Unfortunately, the default response generally is, "Well, let's look at our standardized test scores. . . ."

The real answers to those questions are not found in high-stakes test results but in our classrooms, which are incredibly rich repositories of data waiting to be mined. Why do we give away the responsibility for assessment to test makers and politicians when our daily lives with students provide such authentic data? We have the *real stuff* right in front of us, in situ. Yet we remain silent, and the only data that reach administrators' and the public's eyes are high-stakes test scores, snapshots of a few days in time rather than the year in motion. Teachers need to stop being complicit in this default thinking.

Cochran-Smith and Lytle (1993) have argued for many years that teachers must undertake systematic and intentional inquiry into their practices and become teacher-researchers. Teacher-research, with its data collection methods of *observation, interviewing,* and *artifact analysis,* is a direct match with our lives in the classroom: Every day we *observe* our students, *talk* with them, and *examine* their work. We must make analyzing this authentic data a systematic and intentional part of our lives.

Roberta's life as a teacher is filled with research questions, things she genuinely wants to know about her students and about her teaching. She regularly gathers data, documenting her classroom practices so that she can use them to inform her teaching and respond to others' inquiries. She is ready to step up with examples and answers when others want to know how her students are doing and what they need.

What's Going On Here?

Melvin Cohn's observation that being wrong is equivalent to an increase in learning is an astute observation not only about scientific experimentation but also about the teaching profession. A lesson gone bad is a clear indication of what not to do in the future, but teacher-researchers take it further. They ask, "What's going on here? What does it mean for the future?"

Late in a September unit on the scientific method, Roberta had an opportunity to deal with three intersecting issues. First, she wanted to see whether her students could apply what they had learned about the scientific method to a new situation. Second, she had recently learned that environmental issues were being featured on the new state science tests. Third, she wanted to give her students more practice with testlike questions. Serendipitously, she found an article on the Internet dealing with autumn foliage, one that did not mention the words *hypothesis* and *proof* but that clearly was based in the scientific method. Seeing a way to address all three issues at the same time, she developed a worksheet to accompany the article (see Figure 6.4).

Roberta was sure the students in her two top sections would do well. Imagine her surprise when thirty-one out of forty-nine students failed. There was one A, and only two B's. She could have said, "Oh well," and recorded the grades. But she wanted to know what was going on. On investigation, she noticed that the questions seemed fair but required not one bit of factual recall; instead, they asked students to move into higher-level thinking and apply their knowledge of scientific method to new text. She also realized *she had not taught her students how to do this*. Instead, she had fallen prey to assumptive teaching, assuming that *someone else* had taught them how to reason and apply.

When she returned the assignment, these high-achieving students, accustomed to nothing but A's and B's, panicked. She asked them why the task was so difficult. "It wasn't fair! The article never mentioned anything about a hypothesis or a control group or . . . !" Roberta asked them to dig deeper, until they realized the assignment had not asked them to regurgitate information but rather to think about and apply that information.

Roberta told them she was not going to record the grades for this assignment, because they had shown her that she had work to do. She was going to focus more

Scientific Method and Autumn Foliage

Directions: First, read over the entire article. Then, reread it and answer the following questions as you go along. Circle the letter of the best answer.

1. What is the problem being studied?
   a. Why is the tourism rate going down in the autumn in New England?
   b. What is causing the leaves to change colors from summer to fall?
   c. Is climate change causing the foliage to be duller?
   d. Is the nitrogen level in leaves responsible for the red colors?

2. What is the hypothesis of the scientists at the University of Vermont?
   a. Temperature is the reason for the changes in autumn foliage.
   b. Bright autumn colors are due to cold nights followed by warm days.
   c. Cold daytime weather is causing the leaves to be duller in color.
   d. The colors of the autumn leaves are the same as they have always been but the timing is different.

3. "Leaf peepers" are best defined as _____.
   a. scientists at the University of Vermont
   b. researchers in climate change
   c. tourists going to New England in the fall
   d. innkeepers in New England

4. The experiment is supposed to _____.
   a. measure the color pigments in leaves that have been subject to different temperatures
   b. collect leaves to study the colors at various locations
   c. take the temperatures of the environment and record the colors of the trees in the forests
   d. measure the nitrogen levels of red maple trees

5. The control in this experiment is _____.
   a. trees that are kept in a refrigerated box
   b. the equipment used to measure the levels of pigments
   c. trees that are outside all day and night
   d. trees that are brought indoors at night

Figure 6.4. Scientific Method and Autumn Foliage (*continues*)

6. In this article, *pigment* means _____.

   a. color of the leaves

   b. coloring material in the leaves

   c. nitrogen levels

   d. brilliance of the colors

7. Besides being studied by scientists, information on fall foliage is also important to _____.

   a. weather forecasters

   b. climate control specialists

   c. university professors

   d. the tourist industry

8. Why is this study being conducted over a three-year period? Why isn't it being completed in just one year?

   a. They will go to a different location each year.

   b. It will take that long to gather and evaluate all of the data.

   c. More data ensure more accurate results.

   d. Timing of the leaf changes can mess up the results.

9. The article states that scientists are studying "anthocyanin synthesis." From this, you can take *synthesis* to mean _____.

   a. synthetic, man-made

   b. production

   c. break down

   d. red colored

10. When plants are stressed, they are _____.

    a. experiencing a drought

    b. going through color changes

    c. experiencing a change from the normal

    d. not growing very fast

11. *Phenology* is the study of the influence of climate change on the recurrence of annual phenomena of animal and plant life. Give one other study that the USA National Phenology Network may be interested in.

Figure 6.4. *Continued*

attention on reading and reasoning strategies during her science lessons, because process must be developed along with content. That's what learning is about. She told them that she would give this assignment to them again at the end of the year, this time for credit. When she did, the results were much different.

This spring Roberta proctored the state tests in science. Students were allowed to use highlighters to mark up passages in their test booklets. Some highlighted everything on the page, others highlighted nothing at all. Very few seemed to know how to use highlighting in a systematic way. Thinking about her own teaching, Roberta realized she did not teach the use of highlighting at all. Note taking, text boxes, and sticky notes, yes, but not highlighters. She asked her colleagues. They didn't teach highlighting either. She made a note to "develop lessons that include how to use highlighters effectively and document students' progress." Her research agenda for the following year had begun.

We need to understand errors, false starts, and failures in a new way—as part of a learning process, as things to be examined, questioned, and turned into something better. Missteps will happen; they are part of life. To ignore them or write them off with an "oh well" is a mistake. To acknowledge them, investigate them, and make things better is the solution. Roberta shares this life message with her students. She exemplifies Melvin Cohn's words with short clips from *Mythbusters*, one of her students' favorite TV shows, and stories from her own life. Celebrating mistakes is the beginning of a lifelong cycle of learning.

Open-Ended Surveys

Roberta periodically asks her students to assess their learning in relation to the teaching strategies she uses. She takes their input seriously. For example, after using color-coding to help them learn vocabulary, she asked, "When learning the vocabulary of cells and frogs, we color-coded the vocabulary and the drawings. What do you think of this method of learning? Why?" Her classroom is built on trust and mutual respect, and students responded honestly.

- I think this method is good. The colors help me remember. I learned my vocabulary easily. [There were many similar responses.]

- It is helpful because it helps me know vocabulary quicker and better.

- I thought it was helpful because I learned them much faster.

- I think it is cool because if it was boring kids wouldn't pay attention.

- I think it really sticks in your mind and helps you remember.

- It was pretty. I don't think it was different for my learning. But it was better to look at.

- The colors make it easy to find answers in lab. You just match the color to the vocabulary word.

Name (optional) _____

Mrs. McManus' Report Card

CATEGORY	GRADE	COMMENTS
Group work Stations Partners Seating Sharing	A+	It was cool that we could work with our friends and get to know other people better.
Discipline Fair Controlled Helps you learn	A+	The discipline was good it helped with distractions
Reading Reading guides Text-boxes Books Articles Internet	A+	They helped my reading skills improve immensly. Also, they were different ways to learn the same information, variety is good.
Writing Jottings Essays Projects	A+	I like the jottings and that we didn't have very many essays or projects but they allowed creativity which was good
Labs Scopes Genes Bird beak Chemistry Dissection	A+	Labs were good because they were interactive so you could remember what happened better.

Any other comments? Your a great science teacher. I've learned a lot this year and I'll miss you next year ☺

Figure 6.5. Mrs. McManus' Report Card

Example #1. Percent of Students Rating Their Reading in Science Better, the Same, or Worse

QUESTION: Do you think that you read better now than you did in September? (Think about SQ3R, reading aloud, vocabulary lists, reading guides, etc.) Why or why not? Explain.

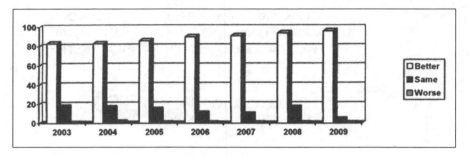

Students listed the following reasons for reading better:

- *Now I think I pay attention more to what I read.*

- *Doing those worksheets and reading slow really helped.*

- *Out of everything, reading aloud and reading guides helped best.*

- *I think I do read better in science because I learned to break apart a paragraph or passage to understand it better.*

- *I think that I read better now in science than I first did because of the reading guides mainly. The color-coding vocabulary helped a lot too.*

Example #2. Number of Students Receiving Failing Grades (1974-2008) in Roberta's Classes

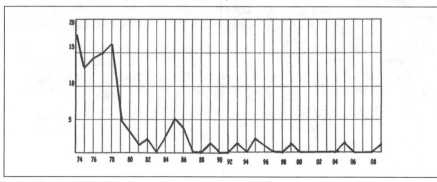

Figure 6.6. Two Examples of Graphing Data

Mrs. McManus' Report Card

One of the highlights in Roberta's classroom happens at the end of the year. Roberta asks students to fill out a report card on her teaching (see Figure 6.5). She allows them to complete it anonymously, without fear of reprisal. She gets serious comments like "jottings gave details and helped me review," "the more variety of sources you used, the more interesting it was," and "the writing helped me from being bored at school." Some of their comments trigger a chuckle: "I think our reading improved a lot, but our class had science early and it was hard to read that early in the morning." "Text boxes and reading guides weren't the funnest but they helped me learn." "Long reading guides hurt my mind." Regardless of their turns of phrase, their input helps Roberta frame how she teaches the next year.

Responding to the Public

Schools exist within a society fixated on Dow Jones averages; our constituents are overwhelmingly business- and industry-minded. Business people want to know the pulse: the market's up, the market's down, the market's about the same. They understand numbers; they like graphs. Test results that can be tracked and graphed fit perfectly into this numerical mind-set, thus their allure. The stranglehold that test makers and politicians have on assessment today consumes millions of dollars and hours of time. The travesty is that every dollar and hour spent on standardized testing (and practice tests preparing for the real tests) is a dollar not spent on books and an hour not spent on instruction.

We need to respond to this mind-set with data drawn from authentic sources—the things that go on in our classrooms—but do so using the numbers and graphs these minds understand. Many things that we do and our students do can be easily converted into charts and graphs (see Figure 6.6). Software on the typical personal computer makes these representations easy to create. Perhaps it's only a pipe dream, but we like to think there will come a day when local school boards "just say no" to these expensive and time-draining tests, confident that their teachers provide them with enough data to know how students are doing.

Teachers so easily fall prey to the notion that *everyone else knows better than I.* Test makers and politicians feed this mania. To this we say, "Rubbish!" *No one* knows our teaching and our students' learning better than we do! Who else is in the classroom with our students every single day? We need to take responsibility for presenting data that matter, data drawn from the authentic fabric of our lives. We must be teacher-researchers.

■ Preparing Future Citizens and Workers

Teachers feel increasing pressure to prepare students for their future lives as citizens and workers. What kinds of thinking will they be required to do? What will future employers want? Are we preparing them for it? Daniel Pink, in *A Whole*

New Mind: Why Right-Brainers Will Rule the Future (2006), takes on such questions. What is most encouraging is that he writes not to educators but to corporate America and the American public, sounding a wake-up call about the kind of thinking and aptitudes needed for the future. What is exciting is that his observations support the kind of good teaching that we—and others—find nonnegotiable. His is a hopeful book.

Pink traces American society's progression through an agricultural age (eighteenth century), an industrial age (nineteenth century), and an information age (twentieth century). Now in the twenty-first century, he finds us at the beginning of a conceptual age, one that will prize aptitudes he calls "high concept and high touch." Although the laborer in the agriculture age was "the farmer," in the industrial age, "the factory worker," and in the information age, "the knowledge worker," the conceptual age will require something much different. The twenty-first century will need workers who are "creators (high concept thinking) and empathizers (high touch thinking)."

The type of thinking required in the first three centuries was heavily left-brain oriented—logical, sequential, follow-the-rules—and it prepared the farmer, the factory worker, and the knowledge worker reasonably well. But the new conceptual age will require workers to operate with thinking skills that are more right-brained—metaphoric, empathetic, and creative. Left-brain thinking will still be needed, but it will not be able to stand alone; thinking that resides in the right brain will be the source of the new and sorely needed aptitudes. In other words, as Pink's title suggests, we need to embrace a *whole* and a *new* conception of the mind.

What senses will be needed in this conceptual age? Pink describes six of them, all high concept and high touch, and all deriving from right-brain function:

- *Design (not just function).* The days of the dull gray trash can are over. Try shopping for one and you will find sizes, shapes, and colors to match any decor. If you are like us, you buy the one that seems to call your name, the one that makes you feel good, the one that says "a classy, tasteful person lives here." It's a functional piece, for sure, but design adds a new richness. Think about stores like Target, product lines like Kmart's home goods collections by Martha Stewart, and so forth. In the age of abundance, those who can design, rather than simply provide function, will thrive.

- *Story (not just argument).* Chapter 1 in this book argues for our nonnegotiables, but we would bet that our arguments came to life for you through story—Donna burning her first CD, Philadelphia city workers cleaning William Penn, Mickey and his Ivy League education, and chemistry teacher John's test of true love. Story is unique to the right brain and it is a powerful pathway to understanding. Increasingly, even medical schools are incorporating narrative medicine into their curriculum. The stories of people's lives tell much about their physical and psychological conditions. It is not extra cushioning; it paves the way to meaning.

- *Symphony (not just focus).* Imagine a CEO stating, "Get me some poets as managers." That CEO was Sidney Harman, multimillionaire head of a stereo components company. Pink contends that poets are the unheralded systems thinkers of our society. They are able to put pieces together, synthesize instead of just analyze, see relationships in seemingly unrelated things, detect patterns, and invent something new by bringing together elements nobody has thought to combine before. Such ability to create symphony—bringing together seemingly disparate ideas into a fresh new whole—is imperative as we traverse a new era.

- *Empathy (not just logic).* Empathy is the ability to put oneself in others' shoes, to sense what is in their heads and in their hearts. It is the intuition that allows a manufacturer to sense what consumers want and need, or a doctor to read what is going on in a patient's life through his face and body language in addition to what is on the chart. It's the nonverbal cues a successful trial lawyer picks up from a jury. Like design, story, and symphony, it derives from the right side of the brain.

- *Play (not just seriousness).* It's hard to believe, but at a Ford Motor plant in the 1930s and 1940s laughter was a punishable offense and whistling, humming, and smiling were regarded as signs of insubordination. The truth is that people rarely succeed at anything unless they're having fun doing it, and humor is noted as a high form of human intelligence. Laughter clubs—yes, clubs devoted to nothing but laughter—are sprouting up all over the world as the physical benefits of the accompanying release of endorphins become more apparent. Even the staunchly left-brain, follow-the-rules U.S. Army has begun using a video game as a recruiting tool. The psychological and physical benefits of playfulness, of joyfulness, are necessary to the human worker and workplace, and studies of successful managers consistently reveal high natural abilities in these two areas. These aptitudes come from the right side of the brain.

- *Meaning (not just accumulation).* Particularly in times of abundance, human beings seek meaning, a reason and purpose for being. Spirituality (which is not synonymous with religion) has moved into the business world as witnessed by findings of the Spiritual Audit of Corporate America conducted by the Marshall School of Business at the University of Southern California (Pink 2006, 223). Although workers in some companies spoke of their hunger to bring their spiritual values to the workplace, executives of those same companies shied away from talking in spiritual terms for fear of offending the religiously diverse population of workers. In companies that acknowledged spiritual values and aligned them with company goals, productivity and performance increased. Reminiscent of Maslow's hierarchy of needs, when physical needs are filled, human beings turn to those things that are self-actualizing, and such things are processed in the right brain.

All of these senses are fundamentally human, and always have been. As Pink observes,

> After all, back on the savannah, our cave-person ancestors weren't taking SATs or plugging numbers into spreadsheets. But they were telling stories, demonstrating empathy, and designing innovations. These abilities have always comprised part of what it means to be human. But after a few generations in the Information Age, these muscles have atrophied. (2006, 67)

Combine these attributes with the ten most important applied skills needed in today's workforce, as identified in a survey of 431 employers (Casner-Lotto and Barrington 2006)—critical thinking/problem solving, oral and written communication, teamwork/collaboration, diversity, informational technology application, leadership, creativity/innovation, lifelong learning/self-direction, professionalism/work ethic, and ethics/social responsibility—and we find still more support for teaching in a different way.

Although in previous ages, logical left-brain thinking developed through lecture, tell-me-what-I-said, and fill-in-the-test-bubbles pedagogy may have been nominally adequate, the future belongs to those with different skills. We need a reconceived set of classroom practices that will help all students develop aptitudes that they will carry over into their lifetimes. The strategies in this book meet this need.

■ What's Next?

You've read this book and many others like it. Clearly, you are taking responsibility for your ongoing professional growth. What's next? Choose one thing that you read about and try it in your classes. Reflect on how it worked. Ask your students for their feedback. Tweak, adjust, and make it your own. Then, try another, and another. Keep track of your data and share it with your principal, even if she or he doesn't ask for it. Find a trusted colleague and share ideas, successes, and failures. A support group is something we all need.

Many things about teaching are not within our control. We don't get to determine our class size, the learning styles and needs of the students who come to us, the budget, and the external mandates that seem ever changing. What we can control is what goes on behind our classroom doors. We hope that we have inspired you to discover (or rediscover) the joy in teaching and remember that the work you do is critical. Your students will benefit greatly from having you as their advocate. And you, as the responsible teacher, will gain a sense of control over this most noble of callings!

Study Guide

Chapter 1 ■ The Nonnegotiables: Six Principles for Teaching

1. As you read the descriptions of the six students at the beginning of the book, did you substitute names of your own students? How do you handle the challenge to educate these students in a diversified classroom of many? Discuss challenges and solutions with your colleagues.

2. In reading the six "nonnegotiables", to which ones do you adhere? Is there one that resonates for you more than the others? Can you add another "nonnegotiable?"

3. Notice how teacher John develops the *before* part of his lesson on hardness of minerals. He hooks kids on an emotional level. What can you do to hook kids more effectively in your classroom? Share ideas.

4. Do you routinely ask students to monitor their learning? Describe/share some methods that you use.

Chapter 2 ■ Demystifying Reading: Helping Every Reader Tackle Texts

1. We are role models for our students. In what ways do we model the fact that we are literate adults? How do you discuss reading with your students?

2. The authors believe that all teachers are teachers of reading. Do you feel confident in your ability to teach reading? Where can you go for more help? How might you better help your students?

3. What strategy (or strategies) offered in this chapter might help your students as they try to make meaning out of text? Try modeling one for them and discuss with your study group how things went.

4. How do you currently handle reading aloud in your classroom? What works and doesn't work with your current method? Are there strategies in this chapter you are willing to try to see if kids will stay tuned in better?

5. In your district, are teachers of content areas included in reading discussions? Are they provided in-service on new techniques or initiatives focused on teaching reading? Are content-area teachers included in your faculty discussions and analyses of reading scores? Are they using the same methods, language, and focal points as the teachers of reading? If not, what might you do to change this so that you have more support?

6. Sometimes we are so well educated in our field of study that we don't understand how others cannot read and grasp the information quickly. Try this in a discussion group: Give your text (textbook, magazine article, internet article, newspaper, and so on) to someone with*out* the same expertise as you. Ask them to identify parts that are unclear. Roberta and Donna have done this and found it eye-opening and very helpful. As teachers, they are then better able to provide scaffolding for those who need it.

Chapter 3   ■ Here Today, Gone Tomorrow? Strategies That Help Students Retain Vocabulary

1. As you challenge students to learn new vocabulary, challenge yourself to develop or adopt a new vocabulary activity for every unit. Vary the strategies to add excitement to vocabulary instruction. Next, enjoy the positive results!

2. How do you differentiate your approach to teaching vocabulary for different types of learners? Do you use different methods? Different time allotments? How do you reinforce your strategies? Share ideas among the colleagues in this study group and increase your repertoire.

3. What types of vocabulary games work particularly well for your students? Discuss why you think they are successful.

4. Which do you find helps your students the most—the vocabulary activities that accompany your teacher's edition of the text or those that you have made yourself? Discuss why. How do they differ?

Chapter 4 ■ Inviting Writing: Helping Students Understand Content

1. In what ways do you engage students to "think out loud on paper"? Share what you do with your group and exchange ideas.

2. With today's emphasis on testing (which includes writing), how often do your students *practice* writing to learn in your classroom? How could you incorporate more opportunities to write?

3. Think of a particular student on your roster who struggles with writing. Could writing that is not for a grade result in a reduction of stress, foster confidence, and promote learning? Can you think of some ways to help that student overcome his/her struggles? Discuss among your group and share ideas.

4. How important do you think it is to give students choice in a writing assignment? Should you assign one topic or several? Give options on the type of writing (poem, essay, etc.)? Or, should you leave the assignment very open-ended? Discuss your beliefs among your colleagues.

5. The act of creation can make people feel good. How do you currently foster creativity in your classroom? Can any of the poetry assignments in this chapter be adapted to your classroom? Share ideas among your group. Try something new and report the results back to the group.

6. One reason that Roberta's poetry assignments are successful is because she is very aware of her students' prior poetry experiences in other grades. Are you aware of the sequence of the writing and language arts curriculum in your district? If not, how can you find out?

7. When discussing writing, the authors say, "Writing expresses complete thoughts and integrates the use of vocabulary in a meaningful way." Do you weave meaningful but nongraded writing into your weekly lesson plans? Why or why not? Discuss responses among your group.

8. Examine your teacher text. Is it a gold mine of thought-provoking questions that can be used for jottings in your classroom? Do you use bell-ringers to start or end a class? If these require only a few words to answer, how can you restructure them to evoke longer written responses from your students?

9. Using "exit slips" as a quick glance into the minds of your young scholars is a way for you to evaluate the effectiveness of a lesson. How can you show your students that their comments have value to both you and them? Brainstorm some ideas and share with your group.

Chapter 5 ■ Many Paths, One Destination: Tapping Into Different Learning Styles

1. How can you add some acting out or drama to your lessons? Donna made a dull section of her textbook come alive through drama. What can you do? Need some ideas? Check out www.teachertube com.

2. In addition, can you hook your students into these dramatic renditions of the curriculum by utilizing new technology? How about a visual review for a unit? Share your results with other classes, schools, and/or countries through technology. Let your pupils be the stars!

3. Try asking your students to play the classic parlor game Charades using vocabulary words.

4. In this chapter, the author's state, "Pop Culture is their world, and frankly, those connections are the ones that are most likely to count in their learning." How can you turn this to your advantage? Discuss with your group, taking advantage of your generational differences and varied musical tastes to learn new ways to connect with students.

5. Is there any particular unit that involves just too much repeated seat work with worksheets? Can you boost its energy with stations set up around the room? Check out pages 99–103 for ideas.

6. "Go To Your Corners", "Ferris Wheel", and "GOGO" are ideas presented that have students up and moving, discussing, and learning. How can you use these strategies in your classroom? Remember, it gives that needed relief to revved up kids who find it difficult to sit for 50 minutes!

7. We've all heard that "A picture is worth a thousand words." With today's technology, we have greater than ever access to pictures. How can you use photographs and art to enhance your curriculum?

Chapter 6 ■ Who Is Responsible for Students' Learning?

1. How do you structure student groupings in your classroom to provide opportunities for movement, different seating, and cooperative partners? Are you providing enough variety? What more can you do?

2. Student sharing of ideas can be powerful. Evaluate the amount of time you allow for that. Brainstorm ways that you can make this a more regular part of your class time.

3. How do you teach your students in ways that encourage metacognition? Are they aware of their learning? Do you provide fix-it strategies that they

regularly use? Brainstorm ways you could help students become more aware of their learning. Try implementing one and then report back to your study group how it went.

4. Need more help for struggling learners in your classroom? Who can you contact in your district and community? Reach out to someone and schedule time for them to work with a student or students.

5. Is there an idea presented in this book that made you cringe and say, "That's not for me!" Is this because of your own learning experiences? Roberta ran into this when she repeatedly resisted the use of poetry in her classroom. Why? Because she doesn't read or write poetry and is convinced that all the poetry genes in her family reside in her younger sister!

   Needless to say, she was pleasantly surprised (stunned actually) when she took the plunge and introduced the Poetry Corner. Not only did her students write wonderful poems but their increased mastery of the vocabulary was evident in their test results! Since they had thought about and played with vocabulary in a creative manner, their comprehension was fabulous.

   Is there a strategy that your students might excel at and enjoy even though you are hesitant to try it? Try that strategy and report back the results. (P.S. Roberta did author one of the poems in this book. Now that's progress!)

6. Looking over Pink's information, what changes do you think educators should make to better prepare students for their adult lives?

7. We encourage our students to be reflective learners and you are encouraged to be a reflective practitioner. Ask for feedback from a person or group—your students, a colleague, an administrator. Discuss with your study group what you learned from this feedback. Use it to become a better practitioner of your chosen craft!

Works Cited

Akmajian, Adrian, Richard A. Demers, Ann K. Farmer, and Robert M. Harnish. 1990. *Linguistics: An Introduction to Language and Communication.* Cambridge, MA: The MIT Press.

Beck, Isabel L., Margaret G. McKeown, and Linda Kucan. 2002. *Robust Vocabulary Instruction.* New York: Guilford.

Bimes-Michalak, Beverly. 1990. Writing Across the Curriculum. Presentation for Berks County Intermediate Unit, Reading, Pennsylvania, 26 March.

Bouchard, David. 1993. *If You're Not from the Prairie . . . .* Vancouver, B.C.: Raincoast Books.

Brown, Margaret Wise. 1949. *The Important Book.* New York: Harper Collins.

Casner-Lotto, Jill, and Linda Barrington. 2006. *Are They Ready to Work?* New York: The Conference Board, Inc.

Cochran-Smith, Marilyn, and Susan Lytle. 1993. *Inside/Outside: Teacher Research and Knowledge.* New York: Teachers College Press.

Cohn, Melvin. 1994. "The Wisdom of Hindsight." In *Annual Review of Immunology 1994,* Vol. 12, edited by William E. Paul, C. Garrison, and Henry Metzger Fathman. Palo Alto, CA: Annual Reviews, Incorporated.

Danielson, Charlotte. 2007. *Enhancing Professional Practice: A Framework for Teaching,* 2d ed. Alexandria, VA: Association for Supervision and Curriculum Development.

Darwin, Charles, and Brian Regal. 2005. Introduction. *The Autobiography of Charles Darwin.* Library of Essential Reading Series. New York: Barnes & Noble.

Dorfman, Lynne R., and Rose Cappelli. 2007. *Mentor Texts: Teaching Writing Through Children's Literature K–6.* Portland, ME: Stenhouse.

————. 2009. *Nonfiction Mentor Texts: Teaching Informational Writing Through Children's Literature, K–8.* Portland, ME: Stenhouse.

Gardner, Howard. 1993. *Frames of Mind: The Theory of Multiple Intelligences.* New York: HarperCollins.

Gregorc, Anthony. 1986. *Gregorc Style Delineator Developmental, Technical, and Administrative Manual.* Rev. ed. Columbia, CT: Gregorc Associates.

Hesse, Karen. 1997. *Out of the Dust.* New York: Scholastic.

Holt Science and Technology Series. 2002. *Cells, Heredity, and Classification.* Austin, TX: Holt, Rinehart, and Winston.

————. 2002. *Introduction to Matter.* Austin, TX: Holt, Rinehart, and Winston.

Kagan, Spencer. 1992. *Cooperative Learning.* San Clemente, CA: Kagan Cooperative Learning.

Kloske, Barry. 2005. *Once upon a Time, the End (Asleep in 60 Seconds).* New York: Atheneum.

Lane, Barry. 2003. *51 Wacky We-Search Reports: Face the Facts with Fun.* Shoreham, VT: Discover Writing Press.

Lytle, Susan L., and Morton Botel. 1998. *Pennsylvania Framework for Reading, Writing, and Talking Across the Curriculum.* Harrisburg, PA: Pennsylvania Department of Education.

Manzo, Anthony. 1969. "The ReQuest Procedure." *Journal of Reading* 12: 123–26.

Norman, Howard A., trans. 1972. *The Wishing Bone Cycle: Narrative Poems from the Swampy Cree Indians.* Santa Barbara, CA: Ross-Erikson Publishing.

Pink, Daniel H. 2006. *A Whole New Mind: Why Right-Brainers Will Rule the Future.* New York: Penguin.

Popham, W. James. 2008. *Transformative Assessment.* Alexandria, VA: Association for Supervision and Curriculum Development.

Raphael, Taffy E. 1982. "Teaching Children Question-Answering Strategies." *The Reading Teacher* 36: 186–91.

Rief, Linda. 1991. *Seeking Diversity: Language Arts with Adolescents.* Portsmouth, NH: Heinemann.

————. 2003. *100 Quickwrites.* New York: Scholastic.

Robinson, Francis P. 1970. *Effective Study.* New York: HarperCollins.

Schaefer, Lola M. 2006. *An Island Grows.* New York: HarperCollins.

Topping, Donna Hooker, and Roberta Ann McManus. 2002. *Real Reading, Real Writing: Content Area Strategies.* Portsmouth, NH: Heinemann.

Warburton, Tom, Dir. 1973, 1997. *Schoolhouse Rock! Grammar Rock.* Los Angeles: Disney Studios.

Weatherall, Peter. "DNA Song." Available at: www.teachertube.com. Accessed October 12, 2008.

Index